WE LIVED IN DANGER

From True Prairie Boy to Royal Regina Rifleman
A Western Canadian's WWII Memoir

VICTOR HEPBURN SMALL, PHD

CONTENTS

PREFACE

"I want to give you some background. There were four Canadian divisions. A division comprises 15,000 people. Two divisions served first in the Italian field. And then joined the European field. When I landed in England, they sent me to the Calgary Highlanders. When I graduated from Sandhurst, they posted me to the Regina Rifles. We learned we were part of a 1,500-truck convoy. I served in the European Theatre of Operations that included England, Holland, and Germany."

— Victor Hepburn Small, April 2020

I, JOANNE, WAS a child during WWII. As a result, I understood what war meant through a child's perceptions. I also realize back then how profoundly Hollywood's post-WWII movies likely coloured those views. Reading Vic's memoir in 2021 helped me recognize, for the first time, that I still held a child's understanding of war. Only then did I come to realize that combat really meant to kill or get killed. That is why Vic's service alone made him a hero to me, though he did not at all agree with me. This was, however, a topic we never fully discussed. So, I can only guess that Vic likely considered those of his wounded, missing, and/or dead comrades certified heroes.

I first met Vic in 1960. It was only fourteen years after he left the military. Yet apparently like other WWII veterans, he rarely spoke about wartime. Especially about his combat experience. I may have gained some insight why, however, when Vic used the word "blackout" in an email he wrote to fellow RR officer, J. Walter Keith. As they briefly discussed their shared recollections of the battle of Leer, they each acknowledged having similarly suppressed or "blacked out" elements of combat.

The content of Vic's memoir roughly divides into four different time periods. One period includes a biographical sketch of his early years in Western Canada written around 2017.

Another includes copies of letters he hand wrote to his family on pale blue, lightweight paper that folded into envelopes. Soldiers referred to those letters as "blue bombers." Vic wrote these letters between the years 1943 and 1945, while still in his late teens and early twenties. His mother, after typing copies of Vic's letters, distributed them to family and friends. Fortunately, I found several more letters after Vic's death in 2021 and added them to his memoir. Then, beginning some sixty-three years after his service, Vic wrote a series of emails between 2009 and 2015. They include personal recollections of a WWII veteran then in his mid-eighties, and answers to the Library of Congress WWII Veterans History Project interview I conducted between April 2020 to May 2020, when Victor was 95 years of age.

I owe a debt of gratitude to the Library of Congress WWII Veterans History Project for providing the questions that ultimately made Vic's memoir possible. Without it, I would not have known how or what to ask him about his military experience, or even ask him to elaborate on the little I knew, based on what he had shared with me over fifty-five years of marriage. For example, I knew he had crossed the Atlantic on board the *Queen Mary* with 15,000 Canadian soldiers. So, I could take the original interview question, "How did you get to your initial point of entry?" a step further when I said to Vic, "I can imagine the Germans would have wanted to destroy a ship like the *Queen Mary* carrying hundreds of soldiers to defend England and defeat Nazi Germany. Did you have any feelings about your safety while on board?" And he said, "A little. We lived in danger."

Our goal, when we began this project, was to record and preserve Vic's WWII experience into a printed memoir for members of our immediate family, though after his death in April 2021, and upon my discovering additional "blue bomber" letters, besides finding the biographical sketch Vic wrote of his early life in Saskatchewan, the idea of posthumously publishing his memoir took flight and made sense. Especially when friends hearing about Vic's memoir told me they would like to read a copy, too. And so, I began a labour of love!

Joanne Wolf Small, July 24, 2022

INTRODUCTION

I WROTE THIS memoir to document and share my experience as a young Canadian soldier serving in Europe during the years 1943 to 1946. And I would like future generations reading it to know or remember that as a former soldier, I believe my story is worth telling. My history includes family letters I wrote, and photographs taken during my service (preserved over sixty years), my biographical family history authored in 2013, and eight emails and additional letters created between the years 2009 and 2015, further recollecting my combat experience. This project began, however, about eleven years earlier, when my efforts to connect to living WWII veterans and members of the Regina Rifles Regiment (RRR) led to my first finding Dolores Hatch, and eventually Kevin Lambie and J. Walter Keith. The letter my wife wrote to Dolores Hatch on September 16, 2009, follows:

Hello Dolores,

I spoke to Sgt. Leonhard von Falkenhausen in the Royal Regina Rifles (RRR) office yesterday. He kindly shared your name and email address. I am writing to you because I offered to help my husband Vic Small see if any surviving veterans from his regiment might wish to exchange stories and share experiences. We live in the US, but Vic remains at heart a Canadian and holds his citizenship. I Googled CA WWII veterans and found the CA Legion webpage and Sgt. von Falkenhausen.

My husband first served a year with the Regina Rifles 3rd Battalion stationed in British Columbia. He had previously accrued five years' service credit with the 64th Battalion Reserve in Yorkton, Saskatchewan. He arrived in Britain in September 1943.

The military transferred him to the Calgary Highlanders until February 1944, and then assigned him to officer training at Royal Military College Sandhurst, where he graduated in December 1944. Vic elected to return to the Regina Rifles when commissioned. They then dispatched him to the front in February 1945. He served in the Army of Occupation in Germany until January 1946. They then discharged him in February 1946 in Regina. We hope to hear from you soon. Thank you!

Dolores Hatch's work as a WWII historian and volunteer with the Royal Regina Rifles honours her uncle Lt. Glenn Dickin, KIA late in the afternoon on D-Day, 1945, serving with the RRR. Kevin Lambie is also a WWII Regina Rifles historian. His work honours a great uncle, Rifleman Donald Morrison, KIA 4 July 1944, having served with the unit in June and July 1944. WWII veteran J. Walter Keith wrote and spoke extensively about his service experience with the Regina Rifles, including mention of my name in *Look to Your Front—Regina Rifles, A Regiment at War: 1944-45*, by Gordon Brown and Terry Copp. Walter and I briefly billeted with the same Dutch family in Holland.

Finally, I wish to credit the US Library of Congress WWII

Veterans History Project for providing sample interview questions, ideas for headings, and a general outline. My wife Joanne Wolf Small conducted the WWII Veterans History Project interview in April and May 2020. She then directly recorded my answers by hand, transferred them into Microsoft Word, and reviewed them for accuracy.

PART ONE

From True Prairie Boy
to Royal Regina Rifleman

CHAPTER ONE

Biographical Details

"A Particular Image of my Boyhood
Remains Clear in my Mind"

1924 to 1942

WHEN I WAS especially young, we used to refer to times past with the question, "What was it like in the olden days, Mom?" Now it befalls me to convey the story of times past in *my* time.

My earliest memory is lying in an upper bunk with my mother as we were on our way "Down East." The second is standing transfixed, looking at a wide escalator, probably in Eaton's department store on Queen Street West in downtown Toronto, trying to figure out how those stairs could just disappear into the floor.

Let me begin by introducing my parents Hazel Catherine Nottingham Small (a homemaker and mother) born in Toronto, Ontario, Canada on February 6, 1899, and Ernest George Small (an optometrist) born in Islington, London, on November 3, 1893, of a large, poor family. Islington, about one and a half miles north of the Thames, appears to have been an industrial area. Male occupations listed included worker, locksmith, iron worker, gas fitter, and plumber. I found my grandfather, Thomas Henry Small, born about 1860, identified as a plumber on Dad's birth certificate. Dad rarely referred to his childhood experiences, though I recall he spoke to me once about having started school in England at four. Discipline was very strict. A mistake led to a rap on the knuckles.

I had little information about exactly when the family emigrated to Canada other than the year because Dad's brother, Uncle Syd, mentioned in a letter how excited he was to find himself aboard the *Lake Erie* in the Gulf of St. Lawrence in 1895. The family settled in Brantford, Ontario.

I understood that Grandpa Small put both Dad and Syd out on farms to work for their keep. And that one reason Dad had given for going to optometry school had been to get away from farm work. Dad had mentioned to me at one point he had worked in an optical lab in Chicago. He subsequently enrolled in the Ontario College of Optometry and moved to Melville, Saskatchewan, a CN Railway divisional point on the main east-west line to Vancouver, British Columbia, in 1923 to set up a practice.

My birth took place in Melville on May 29, 1924. My parents named me after my Uncle Victor, who died in the army at Fort Niagara of the Spanish flu. I am 95. My guess, based on a couple of old photographs, is the house was on Ninth Avenue, which was and probably is still on the northern edge of the town nearly a hundred years later. About a mile north stood a dairy farm run by Hungarian emigrant Steve Makonky, which later loomed large in my young life. We soon moved to a house on Fourth Avenue. It was quite spacious, with a fireplace and a couple of additional rooms alongside the usual dining room and living rooms. My brother George Roger Small (a professor of geophysics at the University of Alberta in Edmonton, Alberta), and my sister Joan Isabelle Small DeLong Mac Donald (a wife and mother), were born there. There was no hospital, no sewage system, and no running water. They all came later.

I found myself enamoured with a new dairy wagon that went by our house. It had a step-down floor in the centre with space for milk bottles above the wheels. I soon attached myself to Tony, the milkman. He was Hungarian and ultimately returned to Hungary. He gave me a parting gift of a package of figs when he left. I had faithfully accompanied him on his daily rounds for many weeks. Gramzie was with us for part of that time. She told me that my behaviour was inappropriate for a person in my position, whatever that was. It did not trouble me or my parents. I spent a lot of time in the barn at milking time. The pipes the men smoked fascinated me. Perforated metal screens covered the pipe bowls to prevent ashes from starting fires in the straw. I sometimes stayed overnight at the dairy. I had an attic room with a small window that looked toward town. It was still there the last time I travelled that way.

I brought home a baby blackbird that had fallen from its nest. I called it Spunky and tried to feed it. It died in a few days. I was sore distressed. That was the first of many stories about me trying to tame or rescue animals.

I must have been about seven when I decided it was time to have a kitten. I know Dad was disapproving, but he packed a kitten into an Oxydol soap box and brought Sandy home. Sandy stayed with us until 1935, when we moved to Yorkton. He disappeared during a cold snap. While in Melville, I used to don my fur-lined leather helmet and fur-lined leather gloves and play with him with no holds barred. He was my feline friend.

Melville was a great place to be a kid. My childhood was wonderful. I loved the prairie and the prairie skies. I loved chokecherry berries and jam, the Qu'Appelle Valley, biking, and anything associated with mixed farming (cows, dairy, and crops). I also loved blue cowbell blossoms. And going to the depot to watch the enormous steam engines come into Melville. Melville had a roundhouse that made it possible for engines to turn around and change direction. Melville Railway Station, built in 1908, was a major station on the Grand Trunk Pacific Railway (GTPR) line. The town in fact took its name from Charles Melville Hays, president of the GTPR, who died on the *Titanic*.

We used to go down to the station to watch the eastbound continental train. Its engine had gigantic wheels. Firemen often shovelled coal into the firebox while the train was still. Brakemen went along the train, checking wheels for overheated bearings. They placed goods from the express cars on express wagons and moved to the express office, which was overseen by Mr. Shearer, who always wore a green eyeshade. Horse and dray moved the goods. There were no trucks in those days. The station had a huge reception area and a telegraph and a ticket office. Steam hissed from radiators in cold weather. Last time I was in Melville, it was an empty shell. What passed for a station was a 10x10 room with bench seats and electric heat. What a comedown! Melville had a couple of other attractions for me. One was what we called "The Ruin." It was an abandoned basement foundation filled with water from spring runoff and absolutely polluted with mosquito larvae. Then there was "The Dam." It was about a mile west of town. The railway built a dam across a valley so it would hold a water supply for the railway. Steam engines had a coal car and a tank car which served the boilers that generated the steam.

The sandpit on the eastern side of town was another attraction. Rainwater collected on the bottom to make for a wading pool. We took off our shoes and socks to go wading. One day, I found I could tie my shoes properly. What makes that day memorable was that when I was tying my shoes, a bullet whizzed close by.

From age four to seven, I spent most summers away on a farm. First, there was a Hungarian family in which the grandparents lived with their children. The grandmother was helping to prepare for spinning. I remember talking with the grandfather as he chopped wood. I collected pigeon eggs and played with the young daughter.

There came a point in our relationship where I concluded the grandmother was leaning on me hard. I employed a subterfuge to get out of a situation which was quite enjoyable otherwise. I phoned home and said I was homesick (never ever true), and Dad came and took me home. No questions. To this day, I wish I could recall the farm's location. It wasn't far from Melville.

When times were good, Mom often entertained and played tennis. We had maids. Dad was away much of the time. In those days, he had a Model T. He travelled to outlying towns and set up temporary offices in hotels or jewellery stores or whatever after mailing announcements of his schedule. In winter, he wore a huge buffalo coat. Cars did not have heaters in those days. Those must have been hard and lonely times. Winters were harsh by comparison with present times.

An event that was significant to our family story is when Melville ceased to be a railway directional point. That killed the town. Then Mom complained of dust collecting on our windowsills. It happens we were on the edge of the dust bowl. The Depression hit. Dad closed his downtown office and took over the two rooms on the side of the house. We had no more maids. Dad was a smart guy. We always had food. Dad planted a large garden and kept bees. I helped him. Looking back, I sometimes wonder how he did it. He had a wife and three children he had to provide for. The only present I received for Christmas was a twenty-five-cent jigsaw puzzle. I also remember looking at an electric train in the window of a shop in downtown Yorkton and wishing I would get it. I did not.

I must have been about ten when Dad opened an office in Yorkton, which is on the Canadian Pacific line to Saskatoon and is almost thirty miles away from Melville. It was four months before he saw his first patient. He slept on a cot in his office. I still have a piece of the curtain to his examining room. What a time it must have been! We never heard a word of complaint about it. The only time we realized how dire the conditions were was when we were in Yorkton. No phone. No car. Crowded in a house on Agriculture Avenue. Dad had proposed that Mom take the kids "Down East" while he tried to survive. Mom would have none of it. The argument became quite heated. And we could hear it. Mom won.

Back to Melville with Dad in Yorkton. Dad commuted back to Melville every Friday during the first winter. I met him at the station with my sled and hauled his bags home. I first attended Central School (a two-room cottage school) in Melville. Each cottage held two grades. So, when younger brother Rog was in Grade 1, I was in the fifth. That separated us by one building holding two grades. We also played in different parts of the schoolyard. Then we moved to Yorkton when I was near the end of Grade 5. I was one of five placed at a kitchen table set at the front of the room. There was no data from Melville. The elementary school had no administrative support. They promoted me and I enjoyed three years of Simpson School before going on to Yorkton Collegiate Institute (YCI). Rog must have moved to Grade 1 in Simpson School. I have fond recollections of my experience in both institutions, because of outstanding and creative principals to whom I owe a debt of gratitude.

When I was older, I stayed at least two summers on Mrs. Stower's farm, about eight miles from Melville on the CN railway, which ends at Fort Churchill on the Hudson Bay. The post office here was in Mrs. Stower's living room. It was called the Brewer post office. The next elevator on the line was McKim, about eight miles north of the Brewer elevator. In 1982, I took an early light picture of the McKim elevator, now gone too. I think the picture is in our cottage bedroom. I treasure it as a memoir of earlier days.

Mrs. Stower must have owned substantial acreage. She had a threshing machine. There was a blacksmith shop with a forge. I liked to crawl into the separator (thresher) to look at all the screens that sifted and sorted the straw from the grain. It stood unused for most of the year.

One of my chores was to get the cows from the northern pasture. I used Old Bob sometimes. He was a horse that showed no signs of hoof trouble while he was in the pasture. Whenever someone mounted him, he developed a rather severe limp.

I took our daughter La to see the inside of the McKim elevator when we were on one of our trips. The agent showed her how the horses pulled the grain wagon so that the rear end hung over a steel grate. The elevator agent opened the door at the back of the wagon and operated a control that tipped it, so the grain fell through the grate to belts below. The horses stamped but did not panic. I have made many a trip from the threshing machine to the Brewer elevator. It was a simple job. The horses knew the way. On that same trip, I found Margaret, a Stower's daughter, operating a turkey farm near Brewer. It was good to see her again.

A particular image of my boyhood remains clear in my mind. On one of our trips to the elevator, we asked Bert Smith, the operator of the adjacent Pool elevator, if we could look at the grain. No one delivered to the Pool elevator in season, so he had time. He poured some of the rich, golden wheat through his hands and said, in an admiring tone, "Number One Northern!" It was beautiful to behold.

I must go on about threshing. It was a wondrous time! The weather was usually glorious. Of course, there have been other occasions in which rain, snow, or frost made for a crop disaster. Men from farms all around gathered to load the sheaves onto the hay racks, haul them to the thresher, and to operate the thresher, now powered by a belt run from gasoline tractors. Work was from dawn to dusk. The ladies brought coffee (and cream!) by the boiler full to the site for breaks. After dark, there was a big spread in the house and everyone went to bed—after bedding the horses, of course! It was a hearty and propitious time. They moved the thresher from farm to farm until all was done. Now two people with a combine and a truck can handle the entire operation themselves.

I have a small photo of a threshing outfit in operation. Data on the back located the scene at Rocanville, which is about one hundred miles south and a little east of Yorkton. Steam generated by a boiler heated by wood powered the tractor (probably a Rumely if I remember correctly). I played on abandoned tractors like that from early years until I reached age fourteen. The last one was behind Campbell's machine shop, which lay at the end of Agricultural Avenue in Yorkton. Steam tractors had a fascinating system via pipes operated by hand or mechanically. I liked to turn a crank and move the oil.

Dad had rented a large, unrentable house on the south-eastern side of Yorkton. It was unrentable because it was unheatable.

Dad closed the open fireplace damper, and all was fine. Just across the street stood the transmission towers of radio CJGX, which broadcast cowboy music all day. We could hear music coming from the iron on the stove and the large metal cistern in the basement.

When we moved from Melville, the piano box came with us. I pivoted it into a private zoo with a pregnant rabbit at one end and a pregnant gopher at the other. When the babies came, the mothers put them all into one nest. I stepped out the back door one morning to a scene of carnage. I found all the animals scattered about the backyard, beaten and bloody. Who could have done it? I did not have any idea. To me, it was a monstrous act.

During this period, I joined the Boy Scouts. I was eleven and supposedly beginners had to be twelve. It terrified me they would find me out. Nobody asked. I stayed in Scouts for six years, became a King's Scout and assistant Scoutmaster, and enjoyed several summer camps.

We moved closer into town to a house on Second Avenue. That put me more than a mile from Simpson School and into another school district. Dad petitioned the school board to allow me to complete Grade 8 at Simpson. I had only to hike two miles for the lunch break. I loved that school!

When I was twelve, I answered an ad in the *Enterprise* about the formation of a signals platoon attached to the 64th Battery Home Reserve Core (Armoury, Yorkton, Sask.). A fellow named Ira Fla had organized a signal core. At that age, one could enlist in the reserve. My first experience with summer camp was a ball. The instruction in map reading fascinated me. We went out on night maneuvers and slept on the bare ground and worried about poison ivy. I think I attended four summer training sessions. I most enjoyed being on the phone at the observation post and seeing how close the shells came to the target. At some point, however, Fla just disappeared from my life in Yorkton. So, I picked it up, and they promoted me at age eighteen to sergeant major of my entire battalion. With a hundred and fifty men under my charge.

I do not have many specific memories of my time at the Yorkton Collegiate Institute. I became involved in plays and stagecraft. The principal, Bill Steinson, blessed be he, had instituted a system during which they taught regular curriculum for seven weeks, followed by examinations. They excused students whose grades met a specific criterion from regular studies for three weeks, while the lower-scoring students reviewed the previous work. I enjoyed drafting, metalwork, and stagecraft and taught a class in analytic chemistry. As soon as we encountered organic chemistry, I dropped the idea of becoming a chemist. I also worked a bit (reading a few lines) with radio station CIGX while in high school.

Five of my friends were close to me. Dave Summers (his father was a minister of the United Church in Yorktown); Graydon Carpenter; Eric Nurse (he lived with us for a while during high school), Norma Beck, and Ruth Dulmadge. All have long passed.

I have fond recollections of my experiences at both Simpson and Yorkton Collegiate Institute because of outstanding and creative principals to whom I still feel I owe a debt of gratitude. Following the war, I graduated from The College of Optometry of Ontario. And I later earned a PhD degree in Psychology from the Purdue University in Lafayette, Indiana, USA.

Came Grade 12 graduation and summer tent camp at Dundurn, near Saskatoon. Previous sessions had been in Manitoba, and I dedicated them to artillery matters. Activities involved traditional rifle range work, route marches, and whatever it took to fill in time. I remember the time when I took the coldest shower in my life. The water must have come from melting permafrost. One characteristic of military life was the competition to have the neatest, most uniform set-out tent kits, which were set out each morning. Not a speck could remain in the tents. One got used to it. Tent living is not comfortable.

I received an offer from the federal government providing a scholarship at the University of Saskatchewan in July 1942, shortly after I graduated from high school. And just after serving as sergeant major at Camp Dundee for the 64, Royal Canadian Artillery, and well on my way to accepting an offer for a role in signals in the 3rd Battalion Regina Rifles Regiment, which was mobilizing. I turned the scholarship down. I met Graydon in England during the war. Apparently, Graydon accepted a government scholarship, but the Canadians had run out of bodies and cancelled the scholarship program. Eric joined the navy. After the war, he roamed the seas as an engineering officer. Years later, I found Graydon in California. My wife, Joanne, and I had kept in touch with David and Peg Summers over the years. They later experienced a serious accident in which David suffered a severe brain injury, which left him incapacitated until his death.

Mom (Hazel Small) and Dad's Ford Model T at Devil's Lake, Saskatchewan, 1923.

Snow scene with brother Roger and sister Joan, Melville, Saskatchewan, about 1932.

Freight train leaving Yorkton, Saskatchewan, on a cold winter's day, about 1939.

Different view of the same freight train leaving Yorkton, Saskatchewan.

A two-room Cottage School I attended, one of three built between 1911 and 1922, to cope with Melville, Saskatchewan's overloading public school system, taken about 1930.

Scenic view of Highway 35 and the Qu'Appelle Valley. This major landscape feature runs from west to east across southern Saskatchewan and is of vital importance as it provides water storage, farmland, wetland habitat, woodlands, gravel pits, and ski areas, 1940.

Folks thrashing and harvesting wheat on a farm near Rocanville, Saskatchewan, 1912.

Dad stooking wheat sheaves somewhere in Saskatchewan, 1912.

CHAPTER TWO

Early Days of Service
"I Joined to Fight the Germans!": 1943 to 1944

I WAS EIGHTEEN years old and set out to enlist in Regina as soon as I returned from summer tent camp at Dundurn. Regina, Saskatchewan, was and still is home to the Royal Regina Rifles Infantry "Up the Johns" military headquarters. Dad asked me to delay enlisting, however, until we (my mother, father, brother, and sister) could go as a family "Down East" to meet relatives. All were complete strangers to us three kids, except for Mom's mother, Gramzie or Grandma Nottingham, who visited us over the years in Saskatchewan. This was in wartime, with gas rationing, but Dad had a Nash with overdrive transmission and had saved his coupons.

The trip was an enjoyable experience, though sometimes gruelling. There were long days of travel. One day stands out. Dad had heard that the Hearst-Geraldton section of the Trans-Canada Highway was to be opened on a certain date and timed our arrival so we could be among the first to traverse it. We were, but it was hardly a distinguished crossing. It wasn't ready. There had been a lot of rain. The road was a morass of mud, water, and muskeg. We had no option but to go on. There were no alternate or side roads. It was a wilderness area. Contractors hauled us out time after time. We concluded they must have been contractually obliged to make restitution for the time overrun. So, we may have been the first travellers to cross, but there was no band to meet us at Hearst.

It was Saturday, and after six o'clock. They forbid gas sales after six o'clock. Dad asked the chief of police to intercede, but it was no deal. We had to stay in a dump of a hotel and listen all night to drunken revels on the street. This was northern frontier country then. We took off again the next day and made it to Toronto without difficulty. We visited relatives in Toronto and in Hamilton and went to Durham to see Aunt Hattie, Gramzie's sister. In Durham, I narrowly missed seeing a cousin from Maine with whom I had some correspondence. We crossed Lake Superior by boat on the way back to avoid the Trans-Canada Highway. It was a pleasant experience.

So, when it came time to go, I left behind my parents: my brother Roger, my sister Joan, and our orange cat named Sandy. I joined to fight the Germans. Every living body did the same thing. I knew about some of them personally, like my best friend Dave Summers' brother, Royal Canadian Air Force Flight Lieutenant Arthur Benson Summers, and my former Sunday school teacher's son, Bill Tripp. I think Art may have served in the Middle East. He was later killed when dispatched to England. Bill Tripp committed suicide when he learned his British bride would not return to Canada with him. Veterans from all over Canada came back for the funeral. Bill's father was a WWI veteran, like my father. Dad and I even landed at the same camp—Aldershot—in the south of England. It was a humongous military encampment originally established during the Crimean War.

I first had to take an enlistment test. I think it took a couple of hours. An officer peeked out and called my name when I opened the door. He inquired about my plans and strongly urged that I do not go to the Regina Rifles but enlist in a scholarship program. I would have none of it. He finally agreed and let me go. They enlisted me as a corporal because I had already been running a unit in Yorkton.

We first went by train from Regina to British Columbia—about a two-day trip. They assigned us to the Colonist Car. It was a passenger coach that provided inexpensive long-distance transportation. All had hardwood seats and bunks, though none had cushions. The Colonist Car became familiar to me as I traversed the country. Detailed memories of the many travels from 1942 to 1946 are gone, but recollections of destinations persist. We off-loaded at Calgary, Alberta, and made our way to Camp Sarcee, on an Indian reservation within walking distance of Calgary. It seemed the 3rd Battalion was at full strength when we arrived. I looked at the blackboard and found myself posted as orderly corporal for that evening. I had had some four years' experience in the 64th Field Battalion, RCA, Signals. Strange, but they allowed boys aged fourteen to serve in signals. For two or three summers, I attended Camp in Manitoba serving in signals, and Camp Dundurn in July/August 1942 as battery sergeant major. (Things must have been tough then). Shilo was great fun for a kid, and all business. Dundurn was basic training and devoid of any artillery or signals content.

Fortunately, our 64th permanent force liaison officer, Captain Brown, had recommended me to the 3rd Battalion. On enlistment, I stated that preference, despite the testing officer vigorously opposing my choice, arguing I instead accept a university scholarship.

It was not long before we found ourselves entrained to Courtenay on Vancouver Island, British Columbia. Courtenay is about midway on the eastern shore of Vancouver Island. It was possible to see snow-capped mountains in the west. There was concern that there might be enemy activity in the channels between the mainland and the island. There was even a submarine scare. Fortunately, it was a false alarm, and a blessing. We had not yet organized as a fighting unit. Winter came. It was cold. There was snow in the mountains, and mush and mud on the ground. We lived in tents. They decided we would begin a seventy-mile route march to Nanaimo. The Japanese current warms the southern part of Victoria Island. It was heavy going. It rained. We were cold. We were wet. Colonel Hewitt went ahead with some others and built some fires we could huddle around. I have a photo of CSM Finch lying exhausted in the sun in his underwear and a photo of wet clothing strung out on a tent line in Victoria. They cancelled the march. And instead, they trucked us to barracks on the exhibition grounds in Victoria. I had about thirty men in my unit/company, all from Saskatchewan. God help us if the Japanese had attacked us at that point!

They ensconced the battalion in barracks in The Willows, the exhibition grounds for Victoria. There was a period in which they issued us (dress) uniforms with collars and ties and walking sticks. The sticks just didn't take. I have photos of some of the Bren Gun Carrier people and singles of mortar and rifle work. It shows that something was going on.

Victoria was a most pleasant setting. I found myself promoted to signals sergeant, and responsible for manning an office switchboard, which arrived from somewhere. I detached with a few of my men from Esquimalt, on the edge of the Juan de Fuca Straits. Our charge was to prove the feasibility of setting up signal lamp contact with an airbase in Sydney, British Columbia, located some miles north of Mount Tolmie in Victoria. It was all night work. We slept all day. We found our time at The Willows (reference to the multitude of local willow trees) mainly consumed by familiar infantry training.

Shortly after returning to Regina, came news that they slated some of us to head overseas. We entrained from Victoria and, after a five-day train trip, stopped off at a reinforcement camp near Windsor, Nova Scotia, teeming with troops. They overwhelmed the town. I got to see the notable Bay of Fundy tides, as we stayed a few days before entraining for the docks at Halifax, where we found the Cunard Line's *Queen Mary* waiting for us. We boarded her with about 15,000 others in darkness. God help us. It was freezing cold. We slept that evening on the open deck, shoulder to shoulder, packed like sardines, then indoors on tiers of submarine-type beds the next. I recall it was in August that we left for England. We must have taken a northerly route because it was so cool for August. Then one morning we could see the gray outlines of Ireland on the eastern horizon. Our first point of entry was Glasgow, Scotland. By afternoon, we docked in Gourock, on the Firth of Clyde. Had I any feelings about my safety while on board ship? A little. We lived in danger.

They offloaded us from the ship by lighters. We entrained to Aldershot on an overnight trip and arrived on Sunday morning. Aldershot, a vast military complex and parade grounds, served as the Canadian reinforcement depot. It seemed almost deserted. There were no sentry boxes or military police looking for AWOL soldiers. You would not know that a war was in progress. It turned out we were free on weekends. London was only an hour away. I made the trip frequently from both Aldershot and Brighton in the coming years.

I wandered about, not knowing what to do with myself, and came across Aldershot's Garrison Theatre. The playbill announced the London cast of Noël Coward's *Blithe Spirit* would show that evening. What did I know then? Nada! So, for twelve cents, I bought a ticket and appreciated a first-class performance, in a nearly empty theatre. I thought it was very generous of the cast to give an evening performance for such a sparse audience. While in London, it would be hard to get tickets.

The news for us was that on our arrival, NCOs (non-commissioned officer) from Canada were to be allowed to keep their stripes, referred to by old hands as "saltwater stripes." Before, all new non-commissioned arrivals from Canada found themselves stripped of their stripes. They immediately posted us to different units. About half of our group shipped to Italy. They appointed the rest of us to various regiments. They sent me to the Calgary Highlanders. That posting, and my quarrel with my platoon officer, may have saved my life. We were setting up a mapping exercise for the platoon to do together. I must have said something, I can't think what, but the officer lit into me in a furious tone. I said nothing but betook myself downstairs and requested an audience with our company commander, Major Thompson, to offer me as a candidate for officer training. The major said he would attend to it.

Some months later, they summoned me to a meeting with a group of officers chaired by our battalion commander, known to the troops as "Mad Mack." Someone asked why I wanted to be an officer. I only remember saying that I wanted to attend university after the war. (Not a very noble aspiration for a soldier.) I didn't say I wanted to win the war or whatever else they expected in such circumstances. I learned later that I got the highest score in Saskatchewan on the general abilities test or whatever was administered to new recruits on enlistment. Maybe that helped. I had just turned nineteen. I heard later that our company 21C Captain Johnny Bright had championed my cause. To his memory, I am forever grateful. It opened a new world to me. He was killed in the landing on June 6.

The regiment, encamped on high ground near Peterborough, had a pleasant view of the countryside. The regimental shoemaker immediately commandeered my boots and installed a steel heel and metal studs on the sole. They made a racket on pavement yet served me well.

The next day, we packed up and headed to Brighton, where for a short time, we occupied houses set in residential neighbourhoods. The houses had no heat, no furniture, little light, and no showers. We then moved to the Brighton beachfront, ensconced near Surrey Square, into what had been luxury homes that lined the beaches for miles. The rooms had no heat and no furniture. We slept on palliasses (mattresses filled with straw) on the floor. We took our meals in dark, unheated basements, and paraded on the esplanade fronting miles of beaches. Having just arrived, the military considered us surplus to the normal NCO strength of a regiment. When on parade, we stood at the back of the parade groups. Our immediate presence made us unnecessary and unwelcome. We did, however, become part of the regiment in time.

Life in Brighton involved a one seven-mile route march with rifle and pack a week over the South Downs, chalk hills covered with grass that covered much of Southern England. The regimental pipers, playing for a short while, usually accompanied us. The pipes lent themselves to a cadenced long stride quite different from that of the Rifles which involved shorter more rapid steps.

While on the Downs on a sunny day, we could look at the

southern sky. The sun glinted from flights of American Flying Fortresses setting out for their daylight runs and terrible attrition over Germany. Their losses became tolerable only when newly developed long-range fighters protected the bombers. In the early spring evening, we could watch the darkening sky fill with Allied bombers on their way to night attacks on Germany.

I never adapted to the lifestyle of most infantry soldiers in the "waiting war" era. Quarters were empty at night. Recreation involved mostly going to dance halls and drinking. Period. So, it behooved me to look about. There was a Baptist church just up the hill from where they posted us. The Baptist and United churches used to share summer services in Yorkton and my girlfriend was a Baptist, so for me there was no problem. I took a seat in the pew, not knowing that pews were "owned" by church members. After the service, a couple of families—the Hunts and the Colemans—greeted me and frequently invited me into their homes. They pushed me to meet a student home from Cambridge. Her name was Marge Hunt. She was an education major. Her boyfriend was serving in the Far East and my girlfriend was in Canada, so we had a strictly platonic relationship. I stopped over to Cambridge once while on the way back from Scotland. Marge showed me around the university. I am glad I had the opportunity. When I read of Cambridge, I had a frame of reference. Marge was a good friend. We exchanged a few letters after the war. Her last letter came from Singapore.

When the weather warmed, we went to a full week of night activities in a region near Hastings, a place that intrigued me, as I thought of the Battle of Hastings in the year 1066. Though I never had the chance to explore the area, I always enjoyed night maneuvers. Another break from routine developed in the spring of 1944. They detached a small group of us and sent us to bunk in a long stretch of empty row houses near the channel.

They gave us no duties and left us free to do what we pleased. When I look back, I realize they intended for us to give any spies in the neighbourhood a clue the Canadians were coming to head up a cross-channel invasion to Calais—a chronic and unsupported rumour that continued to persist.

The weather was pleasant. So, on a Sunday, we sat on a hillside overlooking the ruins of Folkestone which had been within range of German artillery. We could see the white cliffs of France across the channel. And we could go to Canterbury, which was not far away. We (Joanne, and I and La) visited Canterbury on a European trip in 1988. We remember eating a scrumptious evening meal. La enjoyed clambering among the ruins while Joanne and I spent more time in the main building. From there, we three went up to London, Wales, and Scotland.

Back in Aldershot, I was returning from a company route march and met our CSM (company sergeant major). He asked if he could have my mattress. It was something I had gotten in Folkestone when stationed with an advance party intended to mislead Hitler into believing the Canadians would land at Calais. The mattress was an improvement over the palliasse. The sergeant major's request was an indirect way of telling me I was on the way somewhere. "Somewhere" turned out to be an officer selection testing site. It was interesting. For three days, we found ourselves interviewed by a psychiatrist, filled in questionnaires, were subjected to team and individual problem-solving activities, and unsolvable problems, swung on ropes across ponds, worked in teams, and so forth. The one that really stays with me was that after climbing trees to a height of forty feet, we faced running across a gap, joined by an eight-foot plank that looked none to secure. We lost some candidates there.

They sent a group of New Zealand and Canadian candidates to what must have been an officers-in-training, finishing school close to Woking. (My father had been in the same area in WW1). We heard a lecture from the principal of Eton College, among others. I can't remember much else. The general idea seemed to be to upgrade our cultural status.

Sometime later, I found myself in Doodlebug Alley. We were atop the Kent Escarpment about ten miles from the south coast and lying on the route between London and Calais, where they launched the buzz bombs. The engines made a sound like a heavy truck. Everybody ducked when the engines cut off. The bombs dived and exploded, inflicting widespread blast damage.

One fine evening, we stood on the edge of the escarpment and watched an enormous display of fireworks on the coast. A heavy barrage of anti-aircraft fire was used to intercept bombs. Fighter planes had little time to down the bombs before encountering the balloon barrage cables. One barrage crew was located a few hundred yards from our encampment. It was very difficult to disable the bombs, although they flew on a steady course and at a subsonic speed. They just kept coming, night and day.

Not long after, I gained admittance to the Sandhurst Royal Military College in Aldershot, for officer training. Buildings were all brick, three stories with outside plumbing drainpipes that froze in winter. Officer's quarters had fireplaces but no fuel. I fondly remember the view of Albuhera, Barossa, and Corunna barracks as I returned from the rail station. They were gone when I returned on a visit about 1985. Officer training at Sandhurst Royal Military College began a new chapter in my life.

Summer tent camp with the 64th Field Battery, Royal Canadian Artillery (RCA), at Dundurn, near Saskatoon, Saskatchewan, July 1942.

Kit inspection layout, Camp Sarcee, Calgary, Alberta, August 1942.

Shaking slush off tents, Camp Sarcee, Calgary, Alberta, November 1942.

First bivouac, long march from Courtenay to Nanaimo, British Columbia, 3rd Battalion, The Royal Regina Rifles, April 1943.

Training activities, Victoria region, British Columbia, spring 1943.

Looking north to Mount Snowdon in the valley where we had our battle training in Wales, December 1944.

CHAPTER THREE

Leave Letters Home
"Ah, but It's Good to Talk to Someone Who
Comes from the Same Burg!": 1943 to 1944

Editorial note: The following are selected letters by the author while on leave from training during 1943 and 1944. They include travels in London and Southern England, Short-Leave Courses and life at Balliol College, Oxford, and air raids on London mid-February 1944.

Hi Folks,

I came into the city with Uncle Ben this A.M. As soon as I left the Strand Station, I headed for 17 Cockspur Street and found that Mel Poulter was on leave as was I, and not due back till the time that my leave ends. Thus, gladly informed, I followed my nose to the Beaver Club, which is just around the corner, and tried to find by phone whether Alan was in town. Some girls I talked to had cheerful voices and had what would appear to be a sisterly interest in Alan's doings, but he was in Gloucester. The time then was about ten o'clock. I decided I might spend the morning more by accompanying a party on a tour of the Houses of Parliament, which was a most happy and wise decision.

We left the club and crossed The Mall, passing then a curious building looking queer, strong, and unusual in the whole. The guide enlightened us by saying it was an additional part of the Admiralty built in the days when invasion seemed imminent. Constructed like the bridge of a warship, composed of reinforced concrete, and so fitted that it could give any attackers a warm reception and to curtail heavy blasts, and well suited to its intended purpose—that of keeping the navy going in spite all that Jerry can do.

When it came time to turn a corner to reach Westminster, our guide stopped us and explained that the spot on which we were standing could always give him assurance that England was safe. He then turned about and as we looked in the line of his arm we saw framed between the wireless masts of the Admiralty, the statue of Nelson that rests on the top of the Trafalgar monument in his honour. To our guide, that represented the security of England.

Shortly after that, we were outside Westminster Hall, and quite near a statue of Cromwell mounted on his charger and brandishing his sword. The sword is bent because of a bomb explosion a few feet away. When the House raised questions the other day about taking measures to have it straightened, it raised a great hullabaloo. To the House, the bent sword represented the spirit of the people of England during the blitz—bent, but not broken. There again, they can draw strength and fortitude from a symbol.

Westminster Hall is the oldest part of the palace because it is the only part of it that was not destroyed by the Great Fire, so that its age is nearly a thousand years. The scaffolding erected inside to facilitate firefighting rather distracted from the impressions of size that would otherwise be there. It is just filthy rich with history.

A side door led us out into the Star Court, on the other side on which we could see the remains of what the Commons had been. Quite a mess, as you have probably seen in photographs. Inside again, and thence to St. Stephen's Crypt, the chapel for the palace. They styled it in semi-Gothic, beautifully adorned, yet possessing an engaging air of simplicity. Everything is so beautifully done that one takes the total effect for granted.

Cromwell, who was a bit of an atheist, used the crypt as a stable during his interim of power. In that function, the ceiling and walls were whitewashed. Many years later, when things had come back to their own, and the whitewash removed, they found well preserved the painting underneath. Queen Elizabeth and her handmaidens made the Alter Cloth. It is still in good repair.

From there they took us into St. Stephen's Hall, used in times past as the Commons. They styled it in the Gothic and ornamented it with effigies of many of the past rulers of the realm.

I think it rather thrilled everyone when we entered the House of Lords, now being used as the Commons. It all appeared as it does in pictures, but pictures can't convey the beauty of the panelling about the room. The red leather benches added colour to it, and incidentally looked quite comfortable, though we could not test them. They showed the seats of the various parties, as were those of Churchill and the cabinet. They regaled us with details of doings of the House, its ceremonies, and traditions. Little did I think in my school days that I'd someday stand in such a place and hear the details all again! Live and learn and believe ever that anything may come to pass.

We continued through the chamber to the Royal Gallery, in which new important works have taken place. They had ornamented it with effigies of former rulers, and paintings of some of the more recent. On the wall opposite was another of equal size, representing Trafalgar. Each took seven years to do. The light was too dim to enable us to examine them, but they told us they considered the artists quite remarkable in their field.

Passing through a door brought us into the Peers' Lobby, the centre of which is the centre of the palace. The mosaics on the walls were outstanding in beauty and they said women made all of them. Harrumph! The Court of Appeals, corresponding very much to our Canadian Supreme Court, was in session and they allowed us to go in for a short while and listen to the proceedings.

Held in the King's Robing Room, now also being as the House of Lords, it was my first view of periwigged peers, and bought to my mind thoughts of mutton stew, because if the wigs aren't woolly, I'll eat my hat!

The brief passage along which we went to the Robing Room had on its walls the most beautiful and realistic paintings I've seen. I am loath to admire paintings termed good unless I like them, and I did that. The pity of it all was there was no time to linger.

We went through part of the Peers' Library to reach the Commons Dining Room. We saw the table at which only Churchill and his Cabinet could sit, but more particularly they brought us to see the exquisite woodcarving executed by a master craftsman who died before he completed the work that some have compared to Schubert's Unfinished Symphony.

A few halls and passages took us to Committee Room 10, which is used by the press. There are sixteen committee rooms in all. In this was a painting of the ceremony interring the Unknown Soldier in Westminster Abbey in 1920 on Remembrance Day. It was interesting to me because it brought up the thoughts which had come to me when I stood by the Tomb.

Further up the hall, we went into Committee Room 16, the largest of them all. It was in this room that Kitchener spoke to the Commons on the evening that he boarded the *Hampshire* and was never seen alive again. They decorated the walls with paintings of events significant to British history.

Since all this had taken much more time than it takes to tell, and possibly because our custodian wanted to bum some Canadian cigarettes, they took us to the Terrace for a smoke. It is on the edge of the Thames and from it one gets a good view of the entire length of the Westminster Bridge. Over this was rumbling a volume of traffic which I had never seen the like of, because previously I had only seen it on Sundays.

Our custodian, having bummed the cigarettes, took us through the Commons Library and into a part of it in which are inscribed on the walls the names of all the speakers that have held office since the beginning of the House, until the present day. To be appointed speaker is no small honour, and after a speaker has completed his term of office, they give a peerage to him.

Time was growing short, so we hurried through the Commons Lobby, all blackened and chipped by the heat of the fire, and into the Cloisters. It is here that we see the origination of red tape. Below the hanger for a member's coat hangs a piece of red tape which was used to hold the member's sword while he was in the House. Probably in the beginning somebody hooked a bit to tie up some papers so that they could stick them into a pigeonhole, and the custom has spread until even the efficient Germans are struggling with yards of red tape.

From the Cloisters they took us into the courtyard just below Big Ben and told some stories about that magnificent old clock which was a fitting end to our travels through this palace. Even to us, who don't place a lot of stock in symbols, Big Ben means something.

Westminster Palace contains over a thousand rooms, so we only saw a portion of it all. What I saw may not be well-remembered or written, but I hope it conveys some of what I felt while I was there.

Luv, Vic

Hi Folks,

I hope you people will forgive my inordinate enthusiasm, but this promises to be a splendid time! Possibly I had better go back to the beginning, which is my arrival here. The train was a bit late, so I arrived after evening had come. My hazy idea gleaned from reading directions a week ago were in no ways clarified by people who I buttonholed for information because they didn't live there either. Such being the case, I followed my instincts (much sharpened since I began travelling over here) and arrived at Balliol College sans further trouble.

At the Porters' Lodge, I picked up the letter directing me to my room, buttonholed an undergrad, and got there tout de suite. Now, as I am writing, warmed by a gas fire and surveying my little room, I am feeling much pleased with this world. I got an added incentive to that feeling because when I found the secretary's office ready to pay my fees, she said, "Canadians no longer pay fees, affective today." It appears, though, that our cheap Mackenzie King must panhandle for more votes over here because there was a hint the government foots the bill.

On surveying the register, great was my surprise and pleasure to discover the script of none other than B/L Carlson of Yorkton, and straightaway, I met Mr. Carlson. Ah, but it's good to talk to someone who comes from the same burg!

Shortly after that, we trouped into the hall for dinner, and it was a most congenial affair. The setting for the meal was a large hall filled with tables replete with genuine silver, goblets, and all the trimmings. Even with nothing to eat, one could well dream up a meal while seated there. The food was excellent, well served, and satisfying.

Following that, we trouped back into the Common Room—and were addressed by the Master of Balliol, who gave us the dope on the course, and much of interest besides. The secretary came after him to tell us the details of our daily routine. He closed his talk with the roll call which emphasised the already apparent fact that we were a cosmopolitan lot, considering our rank, service, nationality, and all. There are Britishers, Canadians, Americans, Czechs, Poles, and Dutch. Most happy am I to report that from Saskatchewan, there are seven, which I consider a fair representation among eighty-three people. When the secretary ended with the words, "Now nothing remains but the beer, " they fell to with gusto. Of course, the Saskatchewan people had a reunion of the first order. We talked about Yorkton, Saskatoon, Carrot River, and Melville for some while.

We mixed about, here and there, talking about everything under the sun and possibly some matters that aren't, for over two hours, when we settled into small discussion groups which included one with a British colonel, an American Air Force Buck Sgt., a Canadian Army Sgt. (me), a Canadian Navy P.O., and a Canadian Air Force A.L.C. We chewed the fat about everything from soup to nuts, exchanging viewpoints, information about our branches of the service, and our own countries. We talked about the post-war world, and anything in fact that interested us. We got a tremendous kick out of the total experience, let me tell you. I feel much more in my element here than when hearing a discussion of the last flight's drunk, or what woman some fellow had out the night before. I just got a great laugh out of the compromises reached between some Canucks and Limeys who are in the same R.A.F squadron. The Canucks agreed not to call the Limeys "Limeys" if the Limeys would not call them Colonials. With the right spirit, people can get together and settle almost anything, it seems.

A scout came into my room this A.M., put back the blackout, woke me up, polished my shoes and answered several questions. My inquiry about where I might get an iron with which to press my uniform was quite a shock to him. Appearances would show that one doesn't press clothes in the Colleges if one is fashionable. The army is not fashionable but was out of luck for getting an iron, so by the end of the course I was assuming a fashionable appearance. I can say that now that I am writing my letters from a rough draft made on this course.

Appearances also show that to be fashionable, one doesn't cut one's hair, either! You never can tell whom you spoke to, because the Master of Balliol you might easily take for a respectable janitor as a distinguished scholar and educationalist. His appearance, and that of others too, belies the learning and ability that he possesses. Just another quaint English custom possibly, or maybe it results from the dearth of irons these days.

Our first lecture this morning was by Professor Goodhart, who belying appearances again, is an accomplished man. He had spent twenty-six years in the States and twenty-six associated with universities on both sides. These experiences remarkably qualified him for his lecture which was "The English and American Character." He contributed significantly to our understanding each and all of us and one another, by telling us of the reasons and conditions for the differences between the English and Americans. The Canadian's position in the topic is that he is half a dozen of one, and six of the other. I shan't go into the details of the lecture, for it occupied several hours but I want to quote Goodhart's opening words when he quoted a French writer's definition of a foreign country. "A foreign country," said he, "is a country in which everything about it is funny, but its jokes." A masterly opening thought, methinks. From there he told us what made the various aspects of the English and American life funny to each other.

Following this lecture, we enjoyed a black coffee interlude in the Buttery. After which, the Master of Balliol regaled us with the story of Oxford and the development of the university, as well as its management. In my humble opinion, it is all a complexity of rules combining present-day ideas and traditions of the past; coupled in some mysterious way by which things here seem to be governed with little visible organization or effort yet have been "muddled through" efficiently. Something simple and clear-cut wouldn't be cricket, I guess.

The afternoon was most enjoyably spent wandering about Oxford or pulling into anything that took our fancy. We found a place where one can have waffles, so naturally we had some. A long confab followed this in my sitting room before dinner, with the other two things—American Air Force Corporal Len, by name, and a New Zealand Sergeant Ron, by name. Ron has spent three years in North Africa, and the eastern part of the Mediterranean, and is here on three months' leave. We just naturally pal around together.

They took the evening up with a dance at Rhodes House. The girls were nice, but definitely though, in the rush of things, one could scarcely have time to exchange more than a few words with any one girl. However, I took home a Scotch lass (to hers, not mine) after the affair ended. That was my first contact with the Scotch over here and was she nice. We just don't stay about anyone's place long enough to get us anywhere, that's all!

For the information of all inflicted, I've come across a most effective antidote for colds. This much I know—yesterday my cold made me feel most miserable; today I am mostly better.

Well, again the honourable and accurate watch shows that the time is in the wee sma' hours of this morning, so I'd better hie me to bed…

Our first lecture this morning was by Mr. Jones on "The Making of the British State." He is to complete it tomorrow. Beginning with Britain in past times, he covered the major events up to the thirteenth century. Much of it I knew, but it was most fascinating and helped to brush away some cobwebs already forming in my memory. I should say that our study of British history is much more thorough than that done by most people over here, and the Americans, too. That seems to apply also to the history of the other nations of the world. Geography is another weak point with many. A woman last night triumphantly told me she had danced with four Canadians—two of them from Toronto and two of them from Ontario. Where Toronto and Ontario were, she had not the vaguest notion.

During the question period, when he discussed the origins of the gentry, the prof told us that during his conversation with a Chinese student, the student mentioned that in his country the bamboo was the mark of the gentleman. When asked why, he explained the reason was, to quote his words, that bamboo, like the gentleman, was "hollow, upright, and empty." Ain't it the truth?

Our second lecture was by Mr. Ridley, and the subject was Shakespeare and the Stage. He gave us a lot of background to

Shakespeare and the Stage and dealt a bit with Shakespeare's characteristics. It was, despite what you may think, a darned good lecture. Of course, I like it all, you may not.

The key feature of the afternoon was a tour of three of the colleges to give us a general idea of what they were all like. The first was Christchurch, in which is the smallest cathedral in England. Its most interesting feature is the design of the ceiling in one part, which is one possessing very little curvature, and therefore requires great ingenuity to set up the stresses properly. The effect is very pleasant, even exquisite. Sir Christopher Wren never could understand how they did it. They built the dining room—or hall—in Christchurch along lines very similar to that of a feudal baron's dining hall. Indeed, it is not improbable that is what it was at one time, but I did not ask its age. One just takes that for granted.

The evening we have most enjoyably passed in the theatre seeing J. B. Priestley's *When We Are Married*. The tickets were complimentary, and the play very humorous, for the plot involves a situation wherein three couples who have gathered to celebrate their twenty-fifth wedding anniversaries learn in events they never married properly. From that fact and its attendant repercussions and complications comes the horror of it all, increased, of course, by the Yorkshire accent.

Here again, I am late, so I'd better stop. Tomorrow brings another day, and what that day brings you shall know shortly…

This day found me indisposed to rise, or desirous of sleeping in. I indulged myself to the extent of twenty minutes, then reluctantly got up; and reluctantly, in fact, as I crawl between the sheets at night, for they are cold! If you member how Alan used to say that his quarters at Oxford were always cold, let me now verify that fact. It is marvellous how cold it can be, despite the fire.

Mr. Jones continued and completed his lecture on the making of the British State. The discussion following it was first rate, for the Americans seemed to harbour the impression that the Dominions were not independent, and that we paid some taxes to the crown over here, and other erroneous impressions. When Len and I went out for coffee and buns, we enlightened each other on questions that had come to each of us about the other's governmental set up. It was most stimulating.

What we had thought might be a dry lecture on the British Law Courts turned out top rate and provided a lot of questions for our lecturer, a local barrister who did at the odd time stutter a wee bit. When he did that, we all wanted to help him most terribly. My gosh! I'm using Limey expressions! Might as well go the whole hog and add "really" in the Oxford accent, of course.

They took the first part of the afternoon up with a visit to the Radcliffe Camera, camera really meaning room. It has a dome very much resembling that of St. Paul's supported by walls and buttresses which go to form the large room which is now used as a reading room. The reason, possibly, that the dome resembles St. Paul's is that a student of Wren's designed it. When we reached the "roof" of the camera and saw all around us the famed "spires of Oxford," I realized that I'd forgotten my camera. Didn't swear, though, which goes to show that I'm growing old, or philosophical.

Following our gander around the top of the building, we went into the Bodleian Library, quite a historical one, and one of the few that gets a copy of every book published in either the United Kingdom or U.S.A.

What most interested me was the exhibit of ancient books and maps that there is in the library. A map of the world made before Columbus was, I shan't say, amusing, but differs from the world as we know it now. The books executed before the printing press are really works of art. Their preparation must have been terribly painstaking and slow.

This evening. Ah, yes, the evening! It began with Len and I having dinner in the Mitre, which claims to be world famous and is undeniably most ancient and still tries to be exclusive. It serves most excellent meals, albeit expensive. Don't fret your curiosity about the girls. The circumstances of our meeting them are unusual, but their backgrounds and characters are above reproach, or they wouldn't be doing the work they are.

The dinner completed, we went to the house of Dr. Ernest Walker, who was before his retirement the teacher of music in Oxford and quite a prominent figure in the world of music. There, they treated us to a most enjoyable evening with songs and good company. You can all vouch for the fact I'm no musician, yet I enjoyed it as much as any. Len and I had quite a long chat before going to bed. His grin, his way with women, indeed his very nature, is like Eric. We hit it off splendidly. If I don't go to bed now, I shan't even be able to get up in the morning. Goodnight!

I nearly missed breakfast this morning, but only nearly. The last event of the course took place in the Common Room and was a topical discussion of a most informal nature. That idea that Canada is strongly feeling her nationhood and power emerged and has a part of great import in post-war affairs became apparent. Like your home, maybe one can only truly appreciate your country best when viewed from afar and compared to others. We Canadians have realized on this course that no matter how much we may dislike our government, there is in it an outstanding efficiency, and a state of organization in our country about which we do not need to be ashamed.

The last morning found me even more reluctant to open my

eyes, probably because of the culminating effect of the previous late evening. However, there are only twenty-four hours in a day, whether one is on leave or no, and on occasions like this, one must make all use of the time we have.

Our first speaker this morning was Professor Coupland, who is the teacher of Empire history at Oxford and particularly well qualified to speak on his subject, which is "India." His knowledge and experience with that country resulted in his being attached to the Cripps mission as an advisor. The lecture was the best and most pertinent to our present-day interests. A good many of the course members have now bought a copy of Coupland's report now submitted to the government in India. It has been a work taking three years, and it's probably the best thing anyone could find to best understand the problems that are rife in India. This lecture, too, possessed another important feature. Innocent though, we discovered we were on the status of Indian affairs; I think the Americans were more so, given their general insistence on immediate self-government, on several erroneous impressions. The prof presented the facts and one could draw one's own conclusions. Certain I am that we did a lot of overhauling of previous ideas.

After a brief rest for coffee, the Town Clerk of Oxford gave us an inside view of local government. It was hard to get at the pith of things because what I read about the university government here applies too.

Immediately after the noon meal, Ron, Len, and I went to Elliston's and had a double order of waffles—a most unusual occurrence apparently—as waffles are a rare thing, and we weren't in the mood to stand on ceremony.

We left the afternoon open for shopping and such, but Sir William Beveridge was speaking at Rhode's House at three, so there wasn't much shopping done. We had been hoping Sir

Wm. was to speak of his plan, but it turned out that he spoke of his recent visit to the States and his impressions gained therefrom. His reactions were interesting to us, particularly considering our discussions during the past few days.

On our way back to the college after the lecture, we stopped in at Blackwell's, probably one of the best bookstores in England. I found the anthology I've been looking for. We literally had to take ourselves in hand, and shove ourselves out the door, because everything there were books that held oodles of promise in the reading and severely tempted us to buy them.

Following a brief interval, which we used having tea, a Polish officer gave us a lecture on his country. He seemed to know its history in the minutest detail from the beginning until the present day, and in passing remarks and illustrations, ably refuted some German claims that we had believed held a kernel of truth. If he put across no more important point, he made us realize the enormous task that lies ahead in the settling of Europe's problems and boundaries. As with India, the solution is difficult, nor indeed, will it be easy to solve.

Len and I have been in my sitting room for some while and writing, and just recently, Ron had come in. Our conversation turned to his experience in Africa. He was with the only outfit that went all the way from Alamein to Tunis, and in that process, he saw a good lot, though he's reluctant to talk. I am afraid that when all this is over and we are back to our units, we are going to come to earth with a fearful bump which won't be in the least pleasant. Len and Ron, I'm really going to miss, for though we have not known each other for long, we've become bosom pals. It has been a great experience.

Len, Ron and I, as has become our daily custom, went to Elliston's for waffles, and talked over things that come to the fore when goodbyes are nearby. Ron will shortly be on his way back to Africa. It was with a heavy heart that Len and I bade him goodbye. He is a grand fellow.

Len and I travelled as far as King's Cross together, then parted, having made an agreement that we shall try to meet again, and in Oxford. We both love this place.

This afternoon, Sunday, Cousin Bren and I have attended a symphony concert in Albert Hall. To do that has been long one of my secret ambitions and its fulfillment was really a pleasure. I shan't tell you what we heard, because when I hear people talking about things in some major or minor, flat, or sharp, I think them most dreadfully highbrow. Anyway, one thing of genuine interest was the fact that the hall is so large that the ceiling was today obscured by the fog that has been prevailing all day! I'm not kidding. The fog, too, had another curious effect, for when Bren and I came out of the Hall I looked across at the Albert Memorial and couldn't help observing how much better the memorial looked when one could scarcely see it! Bren figured I wouldn't last long in Germany if I continued to entertain such opinions.

To get back to the trip, it was disappointing to travel when there was a mist, though it did clear as we neared Newton Abbot. Naturally, the train was late, but that is customary, and one learns to make allowances while in route. I could find Hayhurst's House with no difficulty and found Doris and her mother at home. After getting settled a bit, Doris showed me about Kingskerswell. It hasn't a large population but covers quite an area. It has an old Norman church, but not much else of interest. We are going to run into Torquay tomorrow morning, I think. This house has a very cosy little fireplace nook, and we have spent the evening on maps, talking and reading. Shortly, I shall go to bed and sleep the sleep of the innocent. I felt tired, and I'm not much looking forward to the morrow because all this will end and there won't be anything to write about anymore. Good night!

It was a grand snooze. I slept like a log till half-past nine this morning, and after a hearty breakfast, Doris and I went into Torquay by bus. It is only four miles away. Now, after my visit to this part of the country, I can well understand why Devon is so universally acclaimed for its beauty. I must see it in the springtime.

What nonplussed me a bit was the fact that here, with the enemy just across the water, and often making visitations to remind people of it, one may take pictures of the cliffs and beaches and all whereas on the west coast of Canada, one can't take any pictures of coastal waters at all! Ah, well, it's the fortune of war, but it seems hard when I think of the pictures I did not take back there.

Well, I'll wager by now this letter is awfully close to its maximum weight and, as my leave draws to a close, so shall this record of it. The train isn't the best place in the world to write, even though it stopped for a few minutes.

Luv, Vic.

Editorial note: The following letter appears here in a condensed format due to the length of the original.

Hello folks,

… It's Thursday now, have just finished listening to a German news broadcast in English. I get a terrific kick out of them. On every front, the Germans are slaughtering their enemies, wholesale and repulsing all attacks. Can't quite understand why they must give up places after such successful encounters.

Then there is information designed to buy anti-Semitism, and to separate Britain and the States by mutual distrust. They do not forget to mention the strength of the "Atlantic Wall" in glowing terms. Neither have they missed a single bet in their righteous indignation about the "barbarous" destruction of the Cassian monastery which wasn't being used by Germans at all because Field Marshal Kesselring said so. And then they granted foreign workers (the old bugbears) privileges to those of the German workers. They did not state what those privileges were. One admits that it's darned clever. As a drawing card, they read messages from British prisoners of war...

Hitler put on a first-rate raid for me last night—the heaviest in three years. Uncle Ben woke me up to tell me that the alert had sounded and that the barrage was beginning. I didn't know cause I sleep like the proverbial log in self-defence. It was an awfully noisy affair, because the planes passed right overhead, and were heavily engaged by the ack-ack round about. When things quieted a bit, we went outside to see the sky red in several places with the glow of fire, but they didn't last many hours after the raid had ended. Uncle Ben was quite worried about the bank but learned this A.M. that, while narrowly missed, it was undamaged. One of the staff had his house destroyed by the blast. Now I can say that I've been through a raid of some proportions...

Uncle Ben has just brought in a strip of paper with little pieces of metal splashed on to it. The Jerries drop it in quantity to upset the radio locators. The British started it and I suppose the Jerries thought it a good idea and retaliated in kind. That is all according to the papers, so you can take or leave it. The little enclosed is some that I just found myself with the aid of a flashlight. It differs from that brought in by Uncle Ben but is the same in principle...

Didn't sleep in, because Auntie Mae saw to that, as per instructions. Had time to press my uniform before taking the tube to Charing Cross and no one ribbed me about the pressing. They must get used to my mad Canadian ways.

I toddled merrily along toward the Albert Hall, thinking to arrive nicely fifteen minutes ahead of time, and noticed as I toddled, many cabs seemed to head in that direction too, as well as a lot of other people. When I reached the hall, there were queues at every entrance, so I worried about whether I should get in. I did—went right up to the top of the Hall, in fact, to a gallery where there was standing room only. That had one compensation, though. I met a rather beautiful and interesting Welsh girl, but you aren't interested in such doings, so I'll say no more.

Besides that, of course, there was music—Tchaikovsky's. The Piano Concerto in B-Flat Minor was truly wonderful. The name of the piano soloist I can't recall, but I'll go to hear her again anytime. Couldn't get a program, so that's why I can't tell you much about it.

Later in the evening, I was heading for the tube when the alert sounded, and shortly after, the guns in Hyde Park opened fire. I should have liked to have stayed to watch the fireworks, but I knew that if I did, I might miss the last tube to Edgware. Queer there were a couple of million other people with similar ideas, for I've never seen booking lines, platforms, and trains as crowded before. Everyone just cheerfully squeezed a little tighter and fought their way on or off the train as necessity decreed. It was fun while it lasted, but they told me when they reached here that I missed some of the heaviest gunfire that they had ever heard. Oh well, can't have everything.

Today I must need pack myself up and reorganize, for it is the end of my leave. One will leave no stone unturned to get away on leave as soon as possible, but it's surprising how indifferent one feels towards returning. Guess that's why the army is much more concerned with seeing that you get back than if you leave on time.

Luv, Vic

With the Calgary Highlanders, Brighton, England 1943.

My buddies and I together at Loch Lomond and a Scottish road scene before attending a course at the University of Glasgow.

Uncle Ben Ainsley's photo of the *Queen Mary* while under construction at Clydebank, West Dunbartonshire, Scotland, launched September 1934. I crossed on the *Queen Mary* and docked on the Clyde in August 1942.

Bomb damage to the home of great Aunt Mae and Uncle Ben Ainsley and their daughter, my Cousin Brenda Hastings, in Northeast London.

Statue of Richard Coeur de Lion beside the Houses of Parliament, his sword bent by a bomb explosion a few feet away, symbolizing the spirit of the English people from the blitz — bent but not broken.

CHAPTER FOUR

Wartime Service
"It Took Months Before I Stopped Reacting
to the Sound of Heavy Trucks": 1944 to 1945

MY EXPERIENCE DURING the four months I attended officers' training at Sandhurst Royal Military College encompassed some of the best and worst elements of military schooling. My instructors specifically qualified me to climb mountains. While training to climb mountains was hard, they quartered us at the Royal Hotel near Capel Curig, Wales, close by Mount Snowdon. It was a spectacular country to behold. I also gained specialized active training to use a fire weapon. A flame thrower. But training to climb mountains was harder. In contrast (tongue in cheek), adapting to taking the train—from Aldershot to London—was a lot easier than learning flame throwing or mountain climbing. Which reminds me that one afternoon at Waterloo Station, where a mass of people thronged the concourse, we all heard a doodlebug engine cut off about a quarter mile from the gates, and suddenly, a literal wave of people hit the floor at the same time. Fortunately, we didn't feel the blast. These flying bombs, also called "buzz bombs" and considered one of Hitler's revenge weapons, made a distinctive, unforgettable sound when in flight. It took months before I stopped reacting to the sound of heavy trucks.

A single quality that applied uniformly to all our military instructors at Sandhurst was their competence. They were competent! I especially remember a Captain Keely because he was both competent and calm. Captain Keely's role was permanent force British Army.

The Canadian military provided us with special equipment, including a kit, khaki wool serge battle dress, and a submachine gun called a STEN. I felt honoured to receive a "Sam Browne" belt from Mr. and Mrs. Riches, a British couple from Harrow that gave me a second home when I was on leave. The Sam Browne belt was leather, and two-and-a-half-inches wide, with an added strap, used by officers for dress occasions. The Riches lost two sons, Wilf and Aubrey, May, and June 1944. Mrs. Riches wanted me to wear Aubrey's uniform after he was killed. I first met Wilf in Yorkton while he was in flight training. He was there because Canada had agreed to provide Britain with facilities and training for airmen, and it was geographically safer. Wilf became a squadron leader in the Pathfinder Bomber Force and was shot down while in action. I met Aubrey by chance when I called on the Riches. We went for a walk to Harrow Hill and sat where Byron had sat at one time. Harrow School was on our left. We looked across a broad landscape. Very peaceful. He was killed near D-Day, while acting as an observer for a medium artillery battery supporting Canadian forces. Two sons killed within a month of one another! I brought the Sam Browne belt back with me from the war.

Adjusting to a military lifestyle didn't trouble me at all. Possibly my interest in Scouting and qualifying as a King's Scout some years earlier had something to do with that. "In

Canada," as the scouts define it, "it is the top grade and honour in Scout training, for it literally means what the name implies, a Scout who has passed certain tests of proficiency qualifying him for 'the King's service,' in times of national emergency, and who has assumed the obligation to Be Prepared for such service." It is essentially the same status as an Eagle Scout in the States. And I clearly had enough interest in my early teens to join a signal unit. An upside to that was that the military ultimately gave me credit for my signal core experience, enough that I entered military service as a corporal, later promoted to the rank of lieutenant.

Certainly, there were some enjoyable military service experiences. One time, while on my watch, we were having an inspection for Lieut-General Brian Horrocks. An army photographer appeared and decided he would take two pictures. To my surprise, both were of me *with* Lieut-General Horrocks! Hey, I always thought Horrocks was a very good-looking guy! Another time, I took a comical photograph of Bert Pittaway and George Bevis at Pre-Officer's Cadet Training at Blackdown, England. The same place they stationed Dad during wwi. Bert and George had stuffed themselves into one pair of oversized fatigues. After the war, I looked up Bert Pittaway in Toronto, Ontario, but found he had died. All the fellows in my group were buddies, though I did not go out and drink with them. I was younger—eighteen. They were nineteen and twenty.

Finding friends while serving was easy. Military life encourages a sense of camaraderie. For instance, I met a young medical student in Scotland named Winnifred "Winn" Knox, hosting officers at a reception in Glasgow. She wore a lovely red gown. I came to the reception from our headquarters in Brighton Beach, South England—a long way away. I found time to meet up occasionally with my older cousin, Allan Hepburn Jarvis. Alan had left Canada and was living and working in London. He later went back to Canada, where they appointed him director of the National Gallery of Canada. I often visited and stayed with my Uncle Ben and Great Aunt Mae Ansley, and their daughter, my cousin Brenda Hastings, at their home in Northeast London. I never got to meet Brenda's husband, because I had left England before he came home from service in the Middle East. Unfortunately, a bomb hit my Aunt Mae and Uncle Ben's home, although they kept on living in it. I believe it was their emblem of participation in the war.

Other friends and hosts in England included the Colemans in Brighton and the Burdette family in Harrow, and friend Gene Burdette, in the navy, and stationed a few blocks away on the Strand. The Burdette family kindly offered me hospitality while I was on embarkation leave, and once drove me from Harrow to our embarkation camp near Woking—in total darkness—using up the last of their gas ration. Good people!

When off duty, I typically chose London for recreation. I went to Albert Hall for concerts. I went to the theatre. I went alone, although I occasionally went with Marge Hunt, a genuinely pleasant young woman. London was a war zone. Complete with bomb shelters. So, when necessary, I like everyone else, headed down the steps to a platform in the subway. People stretched out in lines to make room for one and all. It was not too difficult to get around at night by car with no lights, as so few people were out and about.

During the war, I mainly stayed in touch with family by airmail. We wrote letters home on extremely thin sheets of medium blue paper that folded into envelopes. We called those letters "Blue Bombers." It was mostly Mom that wrote back. She was my principal correspondent.

My graduation from Sandhurst Royal Military College took place on December 17, 1944. A dense fog descended on the parade ground. They cancelled the march past. Later, I met Jim Mcullough and his wife, June, and Eric Nurse, a very close friend from Yorkton, for a reunion at Wheatsheaf Pub near Windsor Castle. I was Jim's best man at their wedding. Jim and I were buddies at Sandhurst Royal Military College.

I served in the European Theatre of Operations (ETO) in England, Holland, and Germany. They stationed Canadians on the south coast of England, opposite the French coast, at Brighton Beach. On clear days, we could see the French coast. The Hunts lived next door to the apartments we occupied. I first met the Hunt family (Mr. Hunt was a banker) at a local church. They kindly invited us to socialize with them evenings.

I especially remember waking on June 6 to the sound of planes overhead, as they had already sent me back into the reserve and stationed me in the middle of England on June 6, 1944.

I was in combat for a short time in Northern Germany. I cannot tell you how many times I crossed the Rhine River. In Germany one day, on patrol on route to high ground, suddenly an array of explosives erupted directly in front of us. Had it landed on us, it would have done severe damage! I am not inclined, however, to consider that a matter of good luck. I believe the German soldiers made a mistake. It wasn't a matter of luck. They miscalculated the distance.

I have a photo I took of a bridge on which explosives burned but did not explode, facilitating entry into Deventer, Holland. There was a machine-gun nest in the bushes just at the end of the bridge. The crew surrendered rather than fought. It could have been a bloody affair. You can see the mill that stood near the bridge. We could see the mill in the distance while we waited for the order to advance after darkness fell, and the remains of an 88mm artillery piece after a rocket-firing Typhoon had blasted it. We were being strafed by constant machine-gun fire after occupying some high ground. Suddenly, about twenty feet above my head, a Typhoon appeared, loosed a rocket and disappeared. It was a beautiful sight. The machine fire stopped. We experienced continuous mortar and machine-gun fire the next day after occupying an area outside Deventer. A mortar bomb hit the company headquarters, killed the radio operator and ruined the set, making for great difficulty in communications. I had three very near misses losing my life that day.

While stationed in Holland, I met and made friends with the Vlaming family. They lived in the last house of a row house on the Beatrixlaan 1, Zuilen, a suburb of Utrecht. Another RR, J. Walter Keith and I billeted there together. I much appreciated their giving us milk to drink. On May 29, 1945, I wakened to a beautiful bouquet of red roses on my bedside table with a birthday greeting attached. The Dutch were near starving, but they had their flowers.

A bit more background to the Zuilen-Vlaming story developed soon after the war. I served in Germany with the Army of Occupation. We had quartered a while at headquarters in Northern Germany. Soon after the cessation of hostilities, they then pulled us out of Germany and quartered us in Zuilen to guard German soldiers returning to Germany, and to recognize an army of occupation. They again billeted me with the Vlaming family. Many years later, I re-established contact with them with the aid of a Dutch teacher from Zuilen who had married an American and taught at a school I worked in. I am still in touch (2012) periodically with Vickie Vlaming. She immigrated to Australia after the war.

During the war, I found that both the English and the Dutch people welcomed us. Germany, however, was our enemy. By that time hostilities ceased, it did not feel dangerous to be in Germany, as the German people were no longer a danger. We had pacified the German people! We had completely pacified them!

No. 7 Platoon, "B" Coy, 161st (RMC) OCTU, Aldershot, August 1944.

Final march past of the Third Canadian Army Division took place to
mark the beginning of the Army of Occupation. The Dutch family
I was billeted with noticed the picture of our company passing the
reviewing stand and sent it to me. I am at the left front row, saluting
as I pass. Utrecht, Holland, June 6, 1945.

Canadian Officer Cadets, "B" Coy, 161st (RMC) OCTU, Aldershot, December 1944.

Wearing a uniform and Sam Brown belt bequeathed to me by a grieving mother from Harrow, England, that lost two sons between May and June 1944 and photographed in London at her behest that same year.

CHAPTER FIVE

An Email Written September 18, 2009
"There are Few of us Left Now"

Editorial note: Dr. Small sent the following series of emails (chapters five through eleven) while in contact with two RRR WWII historians, and a fellow veteran between 2009 and 2015.

Joanne has been doing the digging to identify sources of background material and even personal connections with some former buddies and associates. Both of you have been helpful. I feel that I have little to offer. Because I was not part of the regimental ethos that must have existed after the landing, and up to the July period when the pace changed and casualties sorely depleted ranks. This resulted in cross postings with diminution of the geographic connectedness between the troops. What has become clear to me is that when they secured Emmerich (Germany), I found many of the old hands gone. When the 4th Battalion assembled for the occupation, it had drawn ranks from diverse units. The CO had served in Italy. It was not clear that all other ranks were volunteers.

Please allow me to reminisce and wander a little. Looking

over my documents and photographs has called up a flood of memories. I may flesh out the 3rd Battalion data a little. In looking over the roster of officers who had served with the regiment, I recognized some names and can even recall some faces, but not names. The only officers I met post-war were Bill Lyle, who served in Aurich. He later graduated in optometry; practiced in Winnipeg; and joined the faculty of the College of Optometry in Waterloo. Johnny Spanier became a housing inspector in around Yorkton. Jack Edey was in Yorkton at least briefly post-war. He was a sergeant in the 3rd Battalion, and in the same RMC company as me in England. I do not see his name on the roster. Hank Freeman, our dental officer in the field, practiced in Toronto after the war. Mel Douglas was at National Airport in DC when I bumped into him. I understand he came from Canora. I remember him being in Zuilen, near Utrecht, but not in Aurich. Nick Kutney was in the 3rd Battalion. He was a lawyer. It does not look like he affiliated with the Johns following his commission. He died in Toronto in 1975. His son was practicing in Toronto when we visited there years ago. He was a solid member of the Regina crowd in the 3rd Battalion. I felt rather out of place among so many who knew each other. I was the only guy from Yorkton.

Two other people come to mind—Alan Wilde, our bandleader, and Bob Pinder, our med sergeant. They were both older than most. They made it to England and became posted to a holding unit in the Duke of Portland's estate in the midlands (as was I). A truck in the blackout killed Alan. I often wonder what became of Bob. He was a great guy! Enough already!

I have the following if you have interest:

The program for the Service of Thanksgiving, August 1945, in Aurich.

A listing of the officers of the regiment, 6th June 1944 to September 30, 1945.

The Roll of Honour.

A photo of eight Canadian gravesites on the side of the road in Aurich.

A photo of German soldiers' gravesites in Eystrup, Germany. (This was the location of Corps HQ.)

A news report covering the inspection of the RR honour guard for Lt. Gen. Brian Horrocks.

An 8x10 photo of General Horrocks inspecting my platoon with Generals Vokes, and Gibson and others there.

A photo of the provost entourage, for General Montgomery. Lined up in front of the HQ building.

A photo of A Coy lined up for OC's inspection.

A six-page typewritten Regimental History covering the period up to 1945.

Vic

CHAPTER SIX

An Email Written September 21, 2009
"Our Ranks are so Thin and Still Thinning"

I HAD AN extended conversation with Keith yesterday. The geographic districts in which we served matched in some settings. Yet were distinctly separate from others. And widely dispersed in the latter stages of the conflict. It was good to talk to him.

Am I correct to assume that you, Dolores, Keith and Don Breher (I haven't yet placed him) work as an informal network? Exchanging copies of emails and correspondence so all are up to date on new info or events?

I am disappointed to learn that I have had some near misses with recent events. I have limited Canadian contacts, after living over fifty years in the States. Is there an official repository that would assure continuity for the information y'all have gathered? Our ranks are so thin and still thinning. My daughter and grandchildren, like most of their age peers, are almost ignorant of the history of World War II. And have shown little interest. My seventeen-year-old grandson has recently signaled some interest. His commitment to completing his Eagle Scout requirements leaves him no time for diversions.

I have learned that what I have largely matches what you already have though planned to digitize a few photos.

I am curious about Warren Dakin. He was close to Major Mel Douglas and was younger than many officers. I understand he went into law, but that is all I know.

I will fill in the biographical data form. And circulate it to people in my correspondence with email addresses.

It is my impression the information about the regimental history includes almost nothing about the 3rd Battalion and relatively little about the winding-up as we moved into Germany. I may be speaking out of turn. Keith was not part of the 4th Battalion experience, but you may have information from other sources.

Let me know what I might do that would be useful.
Vic

CHAPTER SEVEN

An Email Written October 5, 2009
"I Mentioned Coming Across
an Abandoned 6-Pounder"

I HAD A long chat with Walter yesterday. Walter and I billeted with the Vlaming family in Holland. He helped me to verify the limited experiences I had in the Leer region, Germany. And explained that he had "blackout" experiences, too. I had recalled to him the briefing before the assault on Leer, and the proposed crossing of the river on assault boats without artillery support. I have no memory of the crossing but did recall coming on some firemen trying to put out a blaze, as did Walter. I mentioned coming across an abandoned 6-pounder. He recalled it, too, and losing the crew. I recall waiting through an afternoon while "minnewerfers," or "moaning minnies" landed somewhere, but were no threat.

Walter detailed some heavy action, so I inferred we must have been a reserve company and had come up later. I do not know. My next memory is heading for an advance party to find a bivouac for the night. We slogged through rain and mud and lucked into a big barn with a hayloft. We had hardly settled when word came up (this was May 5) announcing a ceasefire. There was no cheering. Just a great sense of relief.

The next day, I boarded a Jeep, and we headed north. We crossed the canal that was to be a point of resistance. We came to a village. I found a dozen Frenchmen prisoners in a barn. There were a couple of girls (Russian, I think). We heard they worked their fingers to the bone. From carrying milk pails. They had held all as slave labor. They all disappeared quickly.

I found the burgermeister and led him to understand that we were about to be his guests. He negotiated some houses for us. We stayed long enough to attend a service of Thanksgiving at the local church. We headed for Holland. I was back in Germany after the march-past June 6 in Utrecht. We (many of us, that is) headed for home after Christmas.

I could write up many variations of what the post-war occupation experience entailed but wonder if anyone would care now. They composed the 4th Battalion of men from everywhere, it seems, with little or no identification with the Johns. What do you think?

Incidentally, it looks as though the Calgary Highlanders lack a den-mother like you, Dolores. And when I see their casualties exceeded battalion strength, it would be no surprise if there were few survivors now. All for now! Take care, Vic.

CHAPTER EIGHT

An Email Written October 2009
"Our Mess Officer Did an Outstanding Job
of Scrounging Food from the Countryside"

CLEARLY, AT ONE time, I had some photos that I have lost. I have scanned a few that I have kept and am sending them to you for whatever purposes when we come back from the ocean.

I can understand the dearth of information about the 3rd and 4th Battalions, and to get off on the right foot, I will have to explore what you have before I put my oar in.

Dolores: did I mention Lt. Bill Sturbee? He was our mess officer and did an outstanding job of scrounging food from the countryside. Is there anyone out there who served time as an officer in Aurich? I find myself puzzled by my lack of a comprehensive picture of the units there, apart from our own.

All for now. Thanks, Vic

CHAPTER NINE

An Email Written November 22, 2009
"It is a Good Clear Print. If You Need It…"

MY DESKTOP IS now hopelessly out of service. My scans are
on the hard drive. Some people have gotten into deep doo by
trying self cures, according to the internet. Next week I will
call my tech to see what we can do.

I had run off some prints before becoming bogged down.
I shall send them via UPS or USPS if I may have your mailing
address. I am in Bethesda MD, USA. Please let me know if you
do not have my complete address.

Dolores has given me names of a couple of fellows said
to have been with the RRR in Aurich. But none of them have
clicked with me. Even the name of an officer reported to be
our adjutant. I surely knew all the officers after eight months
in Aurich. I never established contact with SS General Kurt
Meyer, who used to pass by my window on his daily walk.

In perusing the stories by Gordon Brown on the internet,
I noted no reference to the massacre of a number or RRR prisoners at Meyer's HQ. Did I miss something? A few years ago, I
watched a short documentary about it on TV.

I am going to check with Keith on the coverage of Deventer. I might have something to add. Many official stories, Brown's excepted, seem to lack a personal element.

I have copies of the Aurich Thanksgiving service and June 6 dance. I think I should send you the originals if you do not have them. Please advise. By the way, do you have a 7x9 copy of Generals Horrocks, Vokes, Gibson and other assorted inspecting my platoon? It is a good clear print. If you need it, I shall have it copied commercially. They can do a good job if they try. Give me the word, Vic.

CHAPTER TEN

An Email Written February 12, 2015
"I Do Not Think I Have Much More Time"

THERE ARE ONLY a few of us left now. Walter's passing was a loss to me personally. We billeted with the Vlaming family in Utrecht. Though we were in the same regiment, forces were so widely dispersed that we had never met before the end of hostilities.

I have been looking over some of the RRR memorabilia today. Nowhere have I even seen mention of the relief of Deventer and Zwolle and on to Leer by a somewhat circuitous route that took us on a northerly route in Holland to the German border. There the Dutch were unfriendly. I gathered they had closer neighbourhood relationships with people on the German side. Walter has showed that he was part of a northerly swing that took him close to water. We were so widely dispersed we hardly knew where we were, much less about the other companies. At a stopover on this side of Leer, we heard we had outrun our artillery and would have no support until they had caught up.

The first story was that we would cross the river in assault boats. In fact, we crossed a bridge in trucks and soon encountered a group of firemen who were dealing with a fire in a building on the road. We took care not to run over their hoses. Shortly after that, we halted and just waited for something to happen. I came across an abandoned 6-pounder. Walter had been ahead of me and has described an encounter in which a few German soldiers had surrendered. We often heard the wobbling sound of minnewerfers. But they did not land near us.

Next day directions came for me to follow a road out of town and extending toward Aurich. Our aim. We slogged along a muddy road and finally came upon a large barn where we spent the night. Came the news the war was over. It gave us a great sense of relief.

We expected to find German resistance in a canal just north of us. There was none. I proceeded north to occupy a village the name of which now escapes me. As mentioned earlier, I found half a dozen Frenchmen, held as slave labourers. There were also two females held on a farm nearby. All the prisoners just disappeared.

I introduced myself to the burgermeister and told him we needed to commandeer some housing for our troops. We held a memorial service at a church in the village. The villagers had their regular service. We followed and had our own service. Somewhere I may have a copy about the order of our service. We stayed there for a week, and then suddenly, entrucked for Utrecht. That is another story. Soon after the final divisional march-past in Utrecht on June 6, orders came, sending some of us back to Germany, as part of the Canadian Army of Occupation (CAOF).

I do not know whether this adds to your background data. Let me know if there might be interest in the Deventer story. Walter must have been LOB (left out of battle) after Emmerich.

I arrived just after Emmerich. I have a copy of a wartime painting representing flame throwers employed to clear some buildings. I took a course on flame throwers in England and received high ratings. But Emmerich was the last flame thrower deployment.

I do not think I have much more time. And what souvenirs I have will have little meaning for my family. It would be no surprise if there were few survivors now. All for now! Vic.

CHAPTER ELEVEN

An Email Written in 2015
"We Settled in with No Guidance from Above"

HERE IS THE broad picture, perhaps more extensive than you would wish in some parts and sparser in others.

We received news of the end of the war on the evening of May 5, 1945. I had led an advance party in a northerly direction after leaving Leer. We slogged through mud all day and ended in a large barn with a hay-filled loft where we stopped for the night. Next day, my orders were to go forward and reconnoiterer the situation. There was no evidence of enemy presence. We came a across a small town with a large church nearby.

While checking about, we came on a dozen French people held as slave farm labourers. My men reported there were female slave labourers on farms. Their fingers worked to the bone from carrying milk pails. We understood we were to keep our distance from displaced people. As related to the Yalta agreement. The Russians claimed that anyone who had surrendered was a traitor and was to be treated like one. They were true to their word. The Allies complied. There lies another tragedy, probably unreported.

I commandeered homes for our company, which came and soon settled in. I sent a truck to Leer to look for some beds. The crew came back with enough beds from a damaged hospital. We settled in with no guidance from above. There was no sign there was an "above." We were killing time. Boring!

We held a memorial church service a few days later. The German civilians exited the church after having their service and the battalion marched in. Ironic! We abruptly departed for Holland and found ourselves in Zuilen. I don't know whether I was there any over fifteen days before we were heading back to Germany after the last march past in Utrecht on June 6, 1945. It was a strange period.

Now to Zuilen. I billeted with the Vlaming household and with Walter Keith. I understand he established a relationship with Geri. Walter had volunteered to go to Japan and so was on track to go home. They selected me for the Army of Occupation without being asked for preferences.

We were free of any regular duties. I sent a crew to find a couple of trees suitable for making a backstop for baseball. I was walking with Vicky as darkness was falling. A man passed us while carrying our backstop poles. I let it pass. Vicky left home in the early morning and returned in the evening.

We could go on a couple of walks. I found her to be simpatico. We said goodbye as she was on her way to Australia. It was a short-lived friendship. It was many years later that we re-established a corresponding relationship. You probably know the story.

I recall there was a group of active and happy young girls moving about in the daytime. We would call it cruising. They often showed up at the Vlamings and then took off for other parts. I recall that in a conversation, someone mentioned a brickyard used as a repository for forbidden goods. No details. I should have inquired further.

I met briefly with a young couple who had returned from Jena after working at the Zeiss factory.

As mentioned before in an email in 2015, I woke up on the 29th of May 1945 to find a bouquet of roses next to my bed. There was a card signed by the family members. I still have it. I do not think I had told anyone about my birthdate. Vic.

CHAPTER TWELVE

A Letter Titled "Deventer"
"We Waited in Darkness"

HI, THANK YOU for your note. I appreciate your thoughts about the lack of general interest in the experiences of vets. I would attribute it to lack of a sentimental basis for indulging in reminiscences which abound among the vets. You and Dolores appear to have a familial or friendship association that binds you. There can't be many survivors of the wartime period now.

I was interested in your mention of Deventer and Zutphen, and to some extent, Leer.

I first encountered Dick Roberts in a small farmhouse where we were bunking for the night, much to the discomfiture of the residents, who grumbled that they had no place to sleep. A medium-range artillery piece fired intermittently during the night. I have no recollection of what proceeded thereafter leading to joining the regiment.

As I recall, Walter did not give coverage to those pieces. My guess is that he was left out or just elsewhere. Walter's story is part of the abiding mystery to me about how we could have been in the same company and so separated in terms of geographics and communication to the end of war and its aftermath up to Zuilen.

I came up to the battalion a couple of days before Deventer action. At first, I delayed us in joining the regiment, which was located west of Deventer. A sniper had killed a popular sergeant-major and there was widespread grief. We waited in darkness. I recall the platoon was eagerly awaiting the return from leave of Rifleman Gipes. I chatted a little with him, though I could not see his face. He seemed a cheerful, gregarious person. Somebody fatally wounded him in the Deventer operation. A shell bounced off a tank and hit him in the forehead. I lost a corporal to a wound in the shoulder in that same operation.

There was another holding period during which they investigated the death of a soldier after a nearby explosion of what appeared to be a mortar shell loaded with gas. Nothing came of it. The reason for the death was not clear.

We were killing time on a road awhile, waiting for the instruction to move. To our front and to the south-west where there was an open view, we could see unarmed retreating Germans moving eastward. Nearby civilians asked for a doctor to assist in a birth. Major Baird, B Company, sent us a group of prisoners to send on. I relieved a surrendering German officer of heavy-duty field glasses. It was all very peaceful. Mel Douglas was our company commander and was with us. I never saw him again until after the war in Zuilen. In the distance, I saw him throwing someone into a canal. Then, many years later, I saw him in the Washington, DC airport waiting room. He was with Ernie Quine, our one-time accountant. I guess he had returned to Canora, which lies about thirty miles north of Yorkton, my hometown.

Mel called an O-group to detail plans for the assault. The

target area turned out to be a cluster of slit trenches in an open area on high ground. The ground fell away eastward to a line of trees, which may have marked a water course feeding into a canal just south of us. Vic.

Post-war photo of the bridge which had burning explosives across
its mid-point and a machine gun nest hidden behind it, though the
bridge never exploded, facilitating our entry into Deventer, Holland,
April 1945.

CHAPTER THIRTEEN

End of Service, 1946
"It Took a Little to Readjust to Civilian Life"

I LEFT ENGLAND from the Port of Liverpool, this time on the Cunard Line ship *Mauretania*, and returned to Nova Scotia, Canada, docking at Halifax. I next boarded the train in Halifax that stopped at the Regina Military Depot, in Regina, Saskatchewan. So, I was back in Regina when my service ended, though I cannot recall the exact day. I overnighted there with my boyhood friend from Melville, Warren Dickey, and his parents. Warren's parents and my parents were friends in Melville. The Dickey family had later moved from Melville to Regina.

I returned home to Yorkton by train the next day. It was February, and it was cold! I had earlier been in touch with Mom, though there was no one from the family at the station to meet me. So, I walked home. I don't recall my brother or sister having any special reaction to my coming home. Or even if anybody else in Yorkton noticed my arrival. Dad came home at five o'clock. There were so many people everywhere, just like me returning from service.

It took a little to readjust to civilian life. I had become especially used to wearing wool battle dress. And recall how warm the house seemed when I first arrived home. The heat took a little getting used to. Then, military service had temporarily interrupted my education. So, my being out of service led to my having a long conference with Mom and Dad. About what I would do now. I understood Veterans Affairs Canada would help support my post high school education, should I choose to go to school. I applied, and then gained admission to the University of Toronto, in Toronto, Ontario, and The College of Optometry of Ontario, also in Toronto.

No, I don't believe military service changed me in any way I am aware of or affected the way I would relate to people. I continued some of the military service-related friendships I made through letter writing. And corresponded for some time with Winnifred Knox. Joanne, La and I later stayed with Winn and her husband while we visited Scotland. I also kept up correspondence with Vicki Vlaming. Vicki had married and moved from Holland to Australia. I corresponded for a while with Vicki's daughter Rose-Maree Verhey, as well. I didn't, however, join any veterans' associations or attend any Regina Rifles' reunions. Yet my wife contacted the Royal Regina Rifles in 2011 on my behalf. I included the letter she wrote at the beginning of my story.

CHAPTER FOURTEEN

Reflections 2020
"Keep Your Head Low!"

IF ASKED, I honestly can't think of any specific "life lessons" I may have learned from the military. Unless, of course, I had a son or daughter about to serve in combat. In that case, I would surely advise them to, "Keep your head low!" Similarly, I honestly don't believe my military service has particularly made me feel any differently about war, or the military. Though I could give that more thought. What I could wish is that more people knew veterans come in all shapes and sizes. Finally, I would like future generations reading my memoir to know or remember that as a former soldier, I believe my story is worth telling.

PART TWO

Leave Letters
"Well, Folks, That's all for Now.
We are on the Move again Shortly"

Editorial note: Part two consists of three letters Dr.
Small wrote home to his parents while on leave from
military duty. Joanne discovered two of the letters,
written in 1945 and lovingly preserved by his family
for over 75 years, shortly after his death in 2021.

CHAPTER FIFTEEN

A Letter Written Home July 1944
"No Sooner had We All Picked Ourselves
Up and Moved Again than Another
Doodlebug Came Over"

Author note: While enrolled in the Royal Military College as an officer cadet and on an educational course at the University of Glasgow, I transcribed this in 02/2005 from a carbon copy typed by my mother, Hazel Small, for local distribution—and it was somehow preserved for sixty years.

Well, folks, this looks like the beginning of another of those long and rambling letters, such as I've written on other leaves. But then, this isn't a leave, so let's say this is another letter. Now I have five days to catch up on, so here goes, beginning with reveille on Sunday early. We (the mob going to Glasgow) had to get up silently and quickly for the rest had had a hard night and didn't have to get up all that day. Having fallen into the duds, sliced off the whiskers, polished the shoes, and so on, we toddled merrily to breakfast. This was an occasion of significant moment, for they honoured us with an egg—the old-fashioned kind with a shell. But to one fellow, that meant little. He gave his egg to someone else because he didn't like an egg without bacon! I've seen everything now!

We boarded a truck and took off for the station shortly after breakfast. We were very much tempted to hold a wings parade right at the station, but the driver was in a hurry to get back. Anyway, we were off to a flying start.

The trip from Waterloo Station to Euston was very interesting because we wanted to see for ourselves what the buzz bombs had been up to. I predict a grand future for the window making industry after the war. There were certainly a lot of windows missing.

We reached Euston with an hour and a quarter to spare and went into the "Y" for another breakfast. It was sausage this time. In addition, we got us some lunches for the trip, and excellent lunches they were, too. There are no dining cars on trains anymore.

By this time, the crowd at the station was something terrific, but the R.T.O. (Rail Traffic Office) had reserved compartments for us. I believe it won't be long before they put benches on the top of the trains to help relieve the congestion. People will travel, even despite it, even when they needn't.

The trip to Glasgow takes about eleven hours. There are few stops and few large centres on the way, so the trip wasn't terribly interesting. They tacked another engine on when we hit the hills, but we lost it on a down grade that followed. It was about half-past eight in the evening when we pulled into Glasgow and had fought our way out of the mob. It was but a short walk to the streetcar stop, but we concluded we were in a wonderful city. There were women everywhere, and they were easy on the eyes. Of course, when you have been living like a hermit for three weeks, anything looks good. To get back to the subject, however, we shortly arrived at the Overseas Club, got sorted out, washed up, and had supper in that order. Then we had something wondrous and rare—some Coca Cola. It tasted rather strange at first, but successive bottles put us on familiar terms again.

It was still light when that was over, so Jack and I went for a walk. We went with the honest intention of seeing the town and walked and walked. There were a lot of kids in the areas we walked through. We walked through the business section and of a residential area. Here the streets were broad and washed marvellously clean by the rain, but the buildings were grimy and dulled by smoke and soot from the ships and shipyards. Our bodies were tired and footsore at the end of our walk and we were happy to go to bed. We all got up early on Monday morning (note the absence of the word "bright") and boarded a couple of busses for Auchincruive, which is the agricultural college for the west end of Scotland. It was a trip of some thirty-five miles and took some while. We arrived without incident, and with no rain to greet us.

We were first shown the poultry sections and some fine-looking chickens. What most interested us, though, were the tiny, downy goslings being "mothered" by old hens. We went from there to see the soil, plant, and animal husbandry departments. They consisted mainly of labs and such, so that I hated to leave them.

We had an extremely interesting lecture from the apiarist and saw the dairying and cheese making departments. We learned that next to Cheddar cheese (I think it is) made in Britain, the consumers' preference goes to Canadian cheese.

After boarding the buses, we stopped at the home of Robbie Burns. They sent us to the adjacent museum after having examined the cottage. A white-haired, bespectacled old Scotsman took us from showcase to showcase and quoted Burns by heart. One boy, following an eloquent spiel, asked the old gent to translate it into English. It took the old man aback a bit, but he translated it, and it still sounded good, or possibly even better, because we could understand it.

Thereafter, we boarded the buses and headed down to the road on a way to see the Burn's memorial—ostensibly, that is. There was a stumbling block at a pub, also named after Burns. Possibly we couldna tell which they wanted us to see, but I know everyone was wonderfully thirsty after a sandwich dinner and that there was a terrific rush of thirst-impelled feet followed by a quiet, broken only by the sounds of slurps and guzzles and admiring remarks concerning the wonderful display of bottles behind the bar. It would be a magnificent place in which to gain a hangover, but there wasn't time. We headed back to Glasgow and had a very hurried supper.

The reason for the hurry was that they wanted us at a reception at the university at seven and we only got back to the club at a quarter to. We got ourselves a wee bit lost on the way but arrived to find the mob imbibing tea and eats. So, we pitched in as heartily as anyone. They had held the speeches off in favour of the eats so that we might all arrive in time to hear them.

About two or possibly three minutes after I blew in, I found myself deeply involved in a conversation with a truly bonnie lassie who turned out to be a medical student and secretary of the Students' Union. If I refer to Win, that will be the person I'm referring to. When we had all arrived and seated ourselves, Sir Hector Hetherington, Principal of the University of Glasgow, welcomed us on behalf of Scotland and the university. Ye shades of Robert Barbour (Robert Barbour was the perennial mayor of Yorkton. He had a thick, Scottish brogue and extolled the virtues of people who come from a small town when he spoke at our Scout banquets). I could close my eyes and imagine that instead of being in Scotland, I was home, listening to the honourable Robert. However, to get back to the subject, he made us very welcome as kinfolk from across the sea. To hear him speak, you would think that Canadians were quite a people. Far be it from me to deny it, but why can't Canadians themselves realize it? It's amazing what you learn about your country after you leave it and particularly on a venture like this.

On the following morning, Tuesday, Professor Mackie, professor of Scottish history and literature, gave our first lecture. He spoke of nationalism and how it had affected the course of history and literature. Then he turned to Scotland, its present problems and how they will affect her future. Until then, very few of us had realized that Scotland has her troubles—in plenty. Och, but it is a guid land!

We heard a lecture by Dr. Kent, a professor of organic chemistry, following a break for coffee. The definition of scientific attitude was told to us by him. He was coldly factual and intensely practical. He gave us an entirely new slant on how science might, if we were not always, or nearly always, adapted to the whims of politics, really result in world betterment. There are deficiencies in the type of general education that he pointed out. The English officers took rather violent exception to what he said, but they could not prove a point. He had them cold at every turn. The Canadians were very much in sympathy with Kent, but we are not so much a product of the education system that he criticized. It was certainly a refreshing period.

We were hungry by that time and proceeded to the Grosvenor Hotel for luncheon with the Glasgow Rotary Club. Once we sat down and talked to some of them, it didn't take long to decide that we liked Scotsmen. They were straightforward men. And very much themselves. They put on no airs, and did not expect any, so we had a jolly time.

The guest speaker was a captain invalided home from Burma. He had been there from the beginning of the Japanese conquest and had some tales to tell. He said we all know too little about Japanese atrocities and gave us a few examples to prove his point. That was the first time I had heard anything about fighting in that area from one who had been there. It sounded gory.

We repaired to the university following the luncheon for a tour of the same. When the smoke or mist doesn't obscure the view, it is on high ground. It differs from Oxford and Cambridge in that rather than being spread all over creation, it occupies one large ground. They made the buildings in Scottish baronial style prevalent about 1800 when the university moved to its present site. Rooms are not large but are very high ceilinged and arched in a style somewhat like, but not as graceful as the Gothic. They showed us the mace of the university in the council room. It is one of the two oldest in the British Isles, made in the fourteenth century. It was beautiful, but I could not help thinking that it would fetch a good price in a hockshop. The army develops one's mercenary instincts!

We went into the archaeological museum later where a little woman showed us about and told a most interesting tale of the old inhabitants of Scotland and of their battles with the Romans. There were sections of Hadrian's Wall, models of forts and all kinds of doodad. We never had time for a gander at the Egyptian section, though while we were there, they took us to the other end of the museum to see some of Scotland's first ships—mere hollowed logs—made about four thousand years ago. Since then, they have come a long way.

After seeing the chapel, they took us to the Hunterian Museum. They housed it in a special building that comprises quite a varied collection of birds, animals, skeletons, corals, and so on, ranging from the simplest forms of life. There I saw a nightingale and a cuckoo. I have yet to hear the song of a nightingale, but at least I have seen one.

They gave us grand circle tickets to a show at one theatre. Win came with me, and we enjoyed it a lot. The settings were good. The jokes were not too dirty, and the girls were good-looking. What more could one ask?

On Wednesday, Dr. Dunlop of Auchincruive spoke to us of agriculture in the post-war world and the effect that the Hot Springs conference may have upon it. We learned things about agriculture in the worldwide sense that we had never expected. We were told of the significant advances made by Russians in that line. One cannot go very far in any direction without learning of the Russians.

Dr. Hearns of the Department of Public Health gave the second lecture. He dealt with social and health problems in Britain as a general example of what the world is up against and then spoke of state medicine and the controversy surrounding it. He, like Kent, was critical of the present setup because much better systems are possible if only that part of politics were the handmaiden of science, rather than the reverse being true.

We attended a reception in the City Chambers by the Lord Provost of Glasgow. Before going any further, I'll translate it into local terms by saying that the mayor held a reception in the town hall. But what a town hall. They built it at a cost of about two and a half million dollars. There are marble staircases, beautiful hardwood floors, and alabaster fireplaces.

The Lord Provost could not attend, so some aldermen and women, and the city treasurer, welcomed us. Said treasurer was replete with a black suit and heavy gold chain, plus an air of geniality that made his words of welcome the more sincere. Then we had tea and talked and tried to entice the CWAC's (Canadian Women's Army Corps) to sit in the lovers' chairs. We went great guns after they introduced me to Sir Ian. They presented all with a book by Robbie Burns and a couple of packages of cigarettes. They do not pull any punches when they put on a tea. It is complete with trimmings.

All good things ended, however, and I set on my way to meet a lady friend's family and all. I got along famously with her father, who is a timber importer and a good head to boot. Her mother is a top-hole cook, and her brother, the young man of the family, is clever and just as contrary as most twelve-year-old boys.

When supper settled, my lady friend and I took me for a walk close to her house. There were lots of shady walks, but you could not walk on the grass. Ah, weel! She took me to a height overlooking the city after the park closed. From there, the view was better than from the university which we could see on the other side. Glasgow has about the same population as Montreal, so it is no small doings.

The first lecturer on Thursday morning was J. F. Arnot, who spoke of drama past, present, and future. He was informative in a good many regards. But he stated that nowhere had the theatre become so decadent as in Canada. We represented all parts of Canada and could not help taking exception to what he said based on our own knowledge. There was a lot of discussion after the lecture, but not much argument.

We heard the Duke of Hamilton speak about the role of aviation in the post-war world. We asked him about the flight over Mount Everest, but no one asked him about Hess. (Rudolph Hess was Hitler's deputy. He flew to Britain from

Germany and asked the duke to intervene to end the war. He died in prison.) The connection between the two only occurred to us afterwards. The duke has certainly been about in his time and has pioneered a lot of things, but for all of that was a rather modest fellow.

Thursday afternoon was probably the highlight of the course. We went to Loch Lomond by bus, driving along the shores or banks, as you will, for miles and miles, stopping here and there on the way. It was lovely and reminded me of many similar places I have seen at home. Our time there was all too short, but most of us felt it would be a grand place to spend a holiday.

We drove along the Clyde for quite some distance on the way back to Glasgow and saw close at hand the ships and docks along its length. There is a heavy concentration of heavy industry that would make good bombing, but Jerry hasn't been around for a long while.

Friday brought the last day of the course. Sir Hector, whom I mentioned near the beginning, spoke to us of democracy in the post-war world. Unfortunately for us, he covered ground that we cadets had covered well before coming to Glasgow, so we dina learn much.

Sir Ian Bolton, whom it was my privilege to introduce, followed Sir Hector's lecture. He discussed youth in the post-war world, particularly from the view of Scouts and allied organizations. He opposed the tendency for compulsory membership in youth organizations, which, although they have their place in war, are of greater use in training youth for war than in the development of excellent character and citizenship so necessary in the days of peace. His talk reawakened in me all the spirit that I used to have for Scouts and all those activities of days gone by. They were great days!

Sir Ian invited those of us who had been Scouts to dinner in his apartment at St. Enoch's Station Hotel. (Sir Ian was a director of Northern Railway.) A major who was or had been a Scottish commissioner for Scouts was a guest. He was a lively old gent, as sharp as they come, and kept us on the go so that we had no time to ask his name. What a man! We fell to talking after dinner. It was a most enjoyable occasion.

I met Win downtown, and we did some shopping before having some strawberries and cream. Yes! I am serious. It cost the equivalent of a buck and a quarter for two servings. It was unquestionably the real McCoy. You cannot find anything like this in Southern England.

After a walk in the park fronting the university, somewhat dampened by the onset of rain, we went to the Grosvenor for supper. The helpings were so hefty that I did not bother to buy a lunch for the train. I figured it would carry me through, even if the train did not reach London until the following noon.

The queues at the station were something outstanding because at that hour, 9 p.m., people were lining up to book tickets when the office opened at 7 a.m. the next day. We had no worries because we reserved our own accommodations.

From Euston, I headed to Edgeware to clean up and press up. I went down to Waterloo to check my baggage before going to a show. The local danger signal sounded, and everyone found what cover was to be had. It was as though an enormous wave had washed across the concourse and they washed people against the walls to the floor. The doodlebug landed and exploded further along the tracks. No sooner had we all picked ourselves up and moved again than another doodlebug came over. The motor cut out, and it fell, landing, and exploding much closer to where we were. I do not wonder that Londoners find it nerve-wracking. Two fellows in my group had had the experience of having a bug explode right close to them, but only suffered minor cuts and a shaking up. We may not go within ten miles of Charing Cross for safety reasons and dependents will not receive any allowance if killed when you should not be there.

I got to Leicester Square after a terrific rush and push in the tubes and saw *The Happy Breed* which has come out just recently.

Well, peoples, that is about all of importance concerning the trip. I will send a blue bomber tomorrow if I get time. 10-14 July 1944.

CHAPTER SIXTEEN

A Letter Written Home March 1945
"The Beginnings of the Castle Go Back Seven
Hundred and Fifty Years and More"

Hello, folks!

Now it begins, again, and for all that is in the earlier letter I might as well begin at the beginning and put in more detail about my visit to Windsor Castle. Memory is but a frail stalk on which to build my tale, so I'll put that which I don't remember for sure. My intention had been to make a few notes while there, but such a thing is more easily said than done, particularly when one forgets to take a notebook.

Possibly I ought to further describe the castle before going into details. It is on high ground near the River Thames in Windsor and commands the whole countryside. Seen from the river, it is very like the massive fortifications portrayed in books of fairy tales. The lightness of the stone makes it seem all quite new, and it's difficult to believe that parts of the castle are seven hundred years old.

A very polite bobby asked me to leave my camera at the gatehouse, and I reluctantly agreed, though it nearly broke my heart to do so, for the exterior of St. George's Chapel took my eye immediately. However, with a broken heart, and without a camera, I went into the chapel, which is undoubtedly one of England's most beautiful. They began building it four hundred and fifty years ago and completed it in its present form much later. Its styling is late Gothic or preferably Perpendicular, though so commonplace a word does it little justice. Perpendicular differs from Gothic in that the ceiling is but slightly curved, and the thrust, instead of operating in the centre of the arch, operates on the slender pillars and delicate walls which are mostly taken up by windows. To take the weight, the pillars curve slightly out at the top like a fan curved outward, hence the term fan vaulting, which is used to describe them.

St. George's Chapel is really several chapels. We assembled in the main chapel and met the man who was to tell the story from the beginning. He did so with great gusto and intonations of voice smacking of experiences ministerial which quite suited the surroundings. There were people from all parts of the Empire there, and Polish, and Czechs, and Americans, and it must have benefited the last-mentioned people that our guide told us the age of nearly everything he spoke about. Apparently, Americans expect nearly everything historical in England to be hoary with age, and far be it from England to disappoint them!

The beginnings of the castle go back seven hundred and fifty years and more. The chapel had its beginning four hundred and fifty years ago, and the work of three sovereigns, each of whom made additions, bringing the chapel to its present size.

In the main chapel it is the pillars and the roof which take the eye for all but four of the side windows are of plain glass. At the back are three stained glass windows taking up the bulk of the space above the main entrance, but they put the glass away for the duration.

The roof above the organ is a masterpiece tracery in stone. In the centre is the Royal coat of arms and grouped about it, coats of arms of twenty-five of the lords of Henry VIII. I don't describe it but can say that probably of all things we saw that day, it made the greatest impression.

Near the back of the main chapel is the tomb of George V on top of which reclines a white marble statue of the king in the uniform of an admiral of the fleet, over which is worn the robe of a member of the Order of the Garter. At the side of the king, Queen Mary will rest when she passes away.

Having looked about there to our hearts' content, we went into the slightly smaller chapel of the Knights of the Order of the Garter. The design is a continuation of that of the main chapel but is further ornamented by oaken towers above the pews. Atop these towers are busts over which are placed the helmets and plumes of the knights. Above these again hang the silken banners in which are woven the coats of arms of the families represented. When a member dies, they remove his headdress and banner, and the bust remains unadorned until the election of a new member to take his place. Besides the banners of the King, the Queen, and the Queen Mother, and the members of the British Lineage there hang the banners of foreign royalty— Greece, Yugoslavia, Denmark, and Sweden. The places occupied by Japan and Italy are now vacant, as the choristers tore down the banners and kicked them out of the chapel—the height of ignominy they can visit upon a member of the order.

Beneath a plain block slab, in the middle aisle, is the last resting place of Henry VIII and Jane Seymour. The mention of Henry VIII anywhere seems to bring smiles. He must have been quite a character and would even so be he alive today.

To the right of the altar is the tomb of Edward VII and Queen Alexandra and on the left of that another kind protected by a set of hand-wrought iron gates said to be of the best existing examples of iron workers' skills.

In the centre is the altar, all beautiful marble behind which is beautifully carved pink marble panelling. On the altar is a cross of gold studded with precious stones, presented by Queen Victoria. All combine to produce a most beautiful effect.

From the chapel they took us to see the rest of what of the castle the public is now permitted to see. We stood on the ramparts looking down to the ground below and thought how much easier it would be to get out than to get in.

We couldn't go to the top of the round tower, which is the most commanding tower of all. Its top stands three hundred feet above the level of the Thames, and from it on a clear day one can see eleven counties and the dome of St. Paul's in London. They surrounded the tower by a flagstaff about 200 feet high on which was that day flying the royal standard, said to be twenty-four feet long and eighteen feet wide. The staff, as you've probably surmised, is of a Canadian Douglas fir. In peace time it used to be scraped and waxed annually.

They then took us to see the entrance to the State Apartments and the quadrangle in front of the Royal Apartments where the changing of the guard takes place. Sorry, but we didn't see the King and Queen waving from a balcony or anything like that. According to the papers, they were busy planting some red oaks in Windsor Grant Park.

Before our wee visit was over, they invited the Canadians to have tea with the superintendent of the castle, which invitation we accepted with alacrity. Why they accorded us the preference, I really don 't know, but it was nice anyway.

There you have it. Pass this on to Butch. Will you please, Mom?

'Bye now, Love, Vic.

113

CHAPTER SEVENTEEN

A Letter Written Home Good Friday, April 7, 1945
"My Letters May Be Less Regular Hence
Forth, but Don't Let That Worry You"

Hello, folks,

It's high time I was writing, but my blue bombers are all in my map case, and that is in my bedroll, so this will have to do for paper. My letters may be less regular henceforth, but don't let that worry you. I'll write as often as possible.

Yesterday morning I chanced to learn that one can make applications for a position in the Department of External Affairs after the war and put my application in pronto. Of course, one must go through university first, but there is no harm in applying early. I've had the idea in mind for about a year now. Competition will probably be tough, but I've nothing to lose by trying. Salary starts at $2,400 a year, so you see what I mean. Alan started the whole idea, and not one can say he doesn't know what it's all about.

I mailed a small parcel home the other day. It may arrive before this letter does. I've been intending to mail the badges for months, but it took a draft to get me to do it in a hurry. Also mailed some photos of Oxford that I've had since going on the course there.

We had a grand send-off breakfast this morning—ham and eggs. I figured that in nineteen months in England, I've had slightly less than nineteen eggs. I guess all this powdered egg I've written about must make up for that. We had green beans for supper tonight and realized with some surprise that string beans are a thing you don't get in the army. Maybe the navy gets them all.

According to the newspapers, the brigade that I'm going to is being kept pretty busy, so I'm hoping my stay won't be long. The pay is going to be complicated because we're paid or credited in dollars and cents, but goes to our account in pounds and shillings, and we draw our money in francs. Some fun, eh?

Say, Pop, now I know where your expression, "Pipe down!" comes from. When it came time for all the soldiers to close their eyes and go sweepers, said command, presaged by the bosun's whistle, came over the ship's P.A. system. It recalled many times in the past when we were making a row upstairs. Another thing that made me smile occurred the other day in a barber shop. I had a haircut and then asked for an oil shampoo. I got it all right. The barber nearly took the top of my head right off—just the way Mom used to when she washed my hair. Had I not remembered that I might have become tempted to haul off and slug him, so maybe it's just as well.

We've had a most interesting time since landing. I can manage with French and this fellow I was with was pretty good at German, and some Belgians know English, so we got along well until we ran into people that spoke only Flemish, and their sign language was sufficient.

As a sign of the times, I should mention what happened in

the pay office as I was drawing some money. A Belgian civilian who worked in the office came up and asked the paymaster if he could go home, as he was feeling quite unwell. After he left, the P.M. said to me, "It's a grim business. They get so little to eat that they can't just work hard." It made me curious about the food situation, so later in the evening we had three cups of tea and four bits of pastry, all for the equivalent of $1.80! I shan't try to buy any more food. They fixed the price of beer, so we stuck to that for the evening. Alcoholic content—nil. Flavour—good.

Continental ideas will take a bit of getting used to. For instance, when you order a beer, a girl comes to sit with you, and if you ask her if she wants a drink, she doesn't have beer—No, Sir—it helps to sell the high-priced stuff, I suppose.

Another thing is the unusual attitude towards public conveniences. Many people seem to use the nearest wall and when you find a spot for "gentlemen" it's as likely as not to be about as open to the world as the—well, one feels bashful about using.

Cleanliness is certainly a characteristic of the people. The streets are clean, the wind is clean, even the furniture is clean in cafés. It's a refreshing change from the dinginess of England. Wallpaper is much more in evidence, too.

We gasped when we saw the shop windows. What, in England, would be considered luxury goods are here to be seen in plenitude. I could get you some real silk stockings, Mom, for the equivalent of nine dollars per pair. Eau de Cologne and various other perfumes, lipstick, powder, rouge and so on are to be seen in plenitude. But, soap, meat, or food, not just apples and vegetables are scarce.

In one café where there was a radio turned in to some BBC dance program, a little girl, who must have been about four and a half or five years old, solemnly danced some very intricate steps for our benefit. She did them very well, and with complete self-confidence. Dancing must have been born in her. Jim gave her some chocolate that he had with him, and she ran off happily. Now I must sign off—just as happily to bed.

It's Easter Sunday, now, and April Fool's Day to boot, so after muster parade, methinks we'll hop aboard a streetcar and see where it will take us. Maybe we ought to wear our new bonnets. Trouble is, it looks as though they might get rained on.

I nearly gave in and bought a small pair of wooden shoes yesterday. They're cute, but they must be hell on hooks. I'd hate to tiptoe on cobbled streets with them.

Well, we climbed aboard what appeared to be a series of streetcars coupled together, which were our equivalent to an interurban train. Travel for Forces is free, so we went about twenty-five miles along the coast towards Holland. It was most interesting, for it made us realize just how much the Jerries put into their coastal defences. The amount of work done on the whole coastline they used to hold must stagger the imagination. Said defences had taken a terrific beating in shots, whether from German demolition or naval shelling is difficult to determine.

We passed through a port that received considerable notice in the last war, and it was entirely disappointing. There was no bustling city as I had expected, but merely the harbour with a few sunken ships to relieve the monotony. I'll tell you the name of the place when I get home, but it's best not to name them now.

Tell brother Rog that if he ever figures travelling to devote twice as much time to French, and to drop Latin. Most of it I've entirely forgotten, but I've remembered considerable French, and wish to goodness I knew more. One forgets verbs and their conjugations, which rather limits the exactitude of tenses in conversation. However, one manages.

The food in the mess is certainly super. Tonight, we had a steak the likes of which I've not seen since leaving home. It was tender and juicy and a joy to the palate. I just hope it lasts.

One could never have thought that today was Easter Sunday. All the shops were open, and things seemed to be just as on any other day. Of course, there were some funny Easter hats, but most people wearing them were too busy keeping on strutting with them. It has been a most windy day.

Well, folks, that's all for now. We' re on the move again shortly, so see that Butch can read this, will you, Mom? Thanks, old girl! (Said with tongue in cheek!) Bye now,

Love Vic.

Canadian Legion liaison officer's photo of me sitting atop the Brigade Administration Building at Brigade Headquarters, Aurich-Oldendorf, Germany, with the Canadian Army of Occupation, 1945.

A Coy Honour Guard, lined up at Brigade Headquarters with the Canadian Army of Occupation, to escort General Montgomery, Aurich-Oldendorf, Germany, 1945.

Members of my platoon, including Calgary Highlanders and Royal Regina Riflemen, which was honour guard at second brigade Headquarters, Eystrup, Germany, 1945.

Lt. General Brian Horrocks inspecting my platoon in Eystrup, Germany, after he and his staff hosted his officers to a lovely evening. Behind me on my left is Major General Christopher Vokes. I had always admired the ability of British officers to relate to lower-ranking officers. September 1945.

Field Marshall Bernard Montgomery and Major General Christopher Vokes leaving the auditorium after delivering a lecture at Brigade Headquarters on the campaign for the west bank of the Rhine. It is the story of *A Bridge Too Far*. I had wandered in the parachute's area landing and saw a mound which said, "Here are 35 British soldiers." As I took their photographs, Montgomery looked directly into my camera and asked me if it was a good camera. Germany, 1945.